DARK DAYS TO CUP FINALS

A SUPPORTER'S STORY OF CRYSTAL PALACE FOOTBALL CLUB 1981-1993

BY

SIMON HIGGINS

© Copyright 2021 Simon Higgins 2021. All rights reserved.

ISBN: 9798734911068.

Published: Self-published through Kindle Direct
                         Publishing.

Email: Higgins15@yahoo.com

Cover: Swindon Town v Crystal Palace Play off
                         Semi Final First Leg. May 1989

                         Provided very kindly by Neil Everett.

Thanks: To all newspapers in the period which

                         formed so much of my scrapbooks and

                         so this book.

Thank-you to everyone who has made my support of Crystal Palace so much fun since December 1972. The majority during 1981 to 1993 are mentioned in this book but if I have missed anyone it will just be a mistake, so please forgive me any oversights!

I feel lucky not only to have made so many long-term friends through the goings-on at Selhurst, but to have experienced the amazing ups and downs and the emotional roller coaster which only football supporters really understand.

Some friends won't be covered by the scope of this book. For example, the two lads who took care of 7-year-old me at the front of the Arthur Wait enclosure as my Dad stood a few rows back. In later years Andy Gibson, Kate Thompson, Graham Carter, Sue Witherow, Colin Moody, Colin Kenny, Stuart Driver, or the "partisan" group who have now sat around of me for years.

Palace are not a club with a wealth of trophies, but the good times come from shared memories, and the hope that may be one day, just possibly, a major trophy will be ours.

This book was written during the lockdowns in 2020 and 2021. I kept scrapbooks for fifteen years and decided to convert twelve seasons into a book, so it is these and my memories on which I have based this book. If there are any mistakes, or oversights, I apologize in advance. If any party feels misquoted, requires credit, text, or photograph's to be removed, or has any other issues with the content please contact me. This was just something to do during covid, so have some sympathy!

There is nothing particularly special about my support of Palace, my stories will be like many, but I hope it's a passable read.

This book is dedicated to both my Dad, John Higgins, and Andy Willmott.

Thanks to my Dad for his help with this book and for holding my hand and taking me to my first game, just a 5-0 win over Manchester United, which led to so much. Also, to my Mum for putting up with tears and moods whenever we lost.

Thanks to Andy Willmott. A fabulous best mate who I feel lucky to have shared so many days at football with, supporting either Palace or following his West Ham. Not to mention fabulous holidays and countless evenings out. He is the first person I text whenever Palace score.

Photographs are kindly provided by Neil Everett, many thanks!

Contents

Chapter	Page
1 Naïve Optimism 1981/82	6
2 Arrival of an old Enemy 1982/83	24
3 News from afar 1983/84	42
4 Ron's gamble 1984/85	57
5 Moving out of the dark days 1985/86	76
6 Legends combine 1986/87	91
Illustrations	110
7 Getting closer to the promised land 1987/88	118
8 Now or never 1988/89	136
9 Hard lessons learned 1989/90	157
10 Potential reached 1990/91	179
11 On the slide 1991/92	196
12 One more point 1992/93	214
Epilogue	233
Statistics	235

Chapter 1: Season 1981/82 - Naive optimism

The previous season had been a total disaster.

Terry Venables after three years of success had left, we had a goal disallowed as the ref who thought the ball had hit a post not the stanchion, had three managers sacked, got relegated by March, crowds had plummeted, the Whitehorse terrace had been replaced by Sainsbury's supermarket, striker Clive Allen who had arrived in exchange for the imperious left back Kenny Sansom had a miserable season and said so, good players had left for QPR to join Venables and to rub our noses in it we suffered a home thumping to bitter rivals Brighton. All this made me the butt of the joke at school. It was impossible to believe it was the same club that had looked so exciting just two seasons earlier with crowds of 30-40,000 and a side lauded as the "team of the eighties".

My Mum, Dad and I had moved to Crawley from Hastings so Dad could be nearer his London office, and he was certainly keen to go to some top division football. I was soon to get used to the ups and downs of Palace. I started with a sensational 5-0 demolition of Manchester United in December 1972, my Mum watching me walk up the road excitedly holding my Dad's hand. A trip to the fish and chip shop on the way home left me assuming all trips to Selhurst Park would be like this. Um, think again!

Two consecutive relegations and we were in the third division. Up stepped Malcolm Allison the manager to lift the gloom, a colourful character with wit, style, and footballing intelligence. He masterminded a fantastic run to the 1976 F.A Cup semi-finals when as a third division team we beat the mighty Leeds United and then Chelsea not to mention Sunderland in the Quarter-Final, all away. Sadly, we barely turned up in a heart-breaking semi-final losing 2-0 against Southampton which me, my Dad, and the stool my Dad made for me to stand on endured at Stamford Bridge. The run at least had made me famous at school "He's the kid who supports that third division club."

Allison and his splendid fedora left at the end of that season having failed to get the club back into division two and suggested Venables took over. That he did and using the excellent youth system Allison had instigated he got us up from Division three with a miraculous last gasp win at Wrexham in 1977. Two years later in front of 51,000 on a sultry night filled with nervous tension we were promoted to the top division with a famous 2-0 win over Burnley. We had a young and exciting team supported by the wily Kember, and the athletic Burridge with his handstand warm-ups in goal.

We started in the first division superbly including thrashing Derby 4-0. This was eclipsed by a magical 4-1 thumping of Ipswich to put us top of the first division and featured a magnificent team goal ending with a spectacular Jim Cannon volley. It's so sad no TV footage exists and it's only in the minds of those lucky enough to have witnessed it on a gloriously golden afternoon at Selhurst. Liverpool, bring them on - who are they!? Sadly, they showed us a few months later beating us 3-0 at Anfield and from then to the end of the season we were very average. We then had the nightmare that was season 1980/81.

But hey, a new season and new hope as my Dad and I got the 1.33 from Three Bridges to Norwood Junction on 29 August 1981 for the season's second division opener against Cambridge. The surprising news was keeping a manager for more than a few months, Dario Gradi. He was appointed by relatively new chairman Ron Noades who used his Wimbledon past to attract him. Gradi said it was best that Allen had left and with that money we acquired Steve Wicks who had a good reputation as a big strong centre back. However, with

Cannon and Gilbert still at the club and still a very reliable partnership many thought the funds should have been spent on a striker. Nevertheless, Gradi felt we had a good team which should challenge for promotion this season. Ron Noades was sounding more reserved talking about how we need income from other streams and not just through the turnstiles. The days of mega TV deals were some way off that's for sure. A new press room had appeared, but not the new centre forward which would have caused far more excitement for 14-year-old me!

New season hopes were boosted with a penalty in the first minute of the season, Paul Hinshelwood put it away into the orange net and added another before half time. With Hilaire a constant threat we played well despite a nervy finish after Cambridge pulled one back from the spot. At the end of the game I was optimistic. However, my Dad had a knowing look indicating that the season wouldn't quite pan out as I was predicting as he couldn't see where the goals were coming from. As we stood by the black gates on a breezy Norwood Junction platform, I knew deep down that he had a sound point as usual. The crowd was 11,612, many paying the £2.50 to stand in the Arthur Wait enclosure. I hoped a few more wins would bring back some of the 20,000 or so who had disappeared over the last two years.

My Dad's prediction seemed reasonable in the next two games. Despite heroics from much criticised keeper Paul Barron, we lost 1-0 at Norwich and then at Sheffield Wednesday.

ITV Sport's "The Big Match" then covered our home game with Charlton, and we put on an impressive performance, with Ian Walsh scoring in each half and new signing Wicks excelling at the back. Certainly, my cousin Graham Harris and his Dad Mick were feeling more positive too with two well-taken goals from open play. The Charlton manager that day was Alan Mullery. He had started the massive rivalry with

Brighton reportedly by throwing a fiver on the floor after an ill-tempered FA Cup second replay in 1976 and saying, "Palace aren't worth that". People relished rubbing his nose in a fine win.

Next up was QPR away. There was a lot of very ill feeling towards them, as they had taken Terry Venables from us as manager and six players all of which would be in our team now – Burridge, Francis, Fenwick, Sealy, Flanagan, and Allen. It was hard to argue that any player we had replaced those with was an improvement!

I had several friends who supported QPR in my class at school and after the last eighteen months as the laughingstock I was desperate for a win. Sadly, my Dad and a large Palace crowd saw us lose to a Stainrod goal in the first half and worse still reliable full back Paul Hinshelwood got injured. The pitch was synthetic and weirdly bouncy. A few weeks later Leicester manager Jock Wallace called for it to be banned, I was pleased our visit was over for the season.

Dr Robert Runcie came along to the next home game against Orient, one dominated by Vince Hilaire. He scored a first half winner but was sent off in a scrap with Billy Jennings in the second half. After losing all three away games so far it was crucial we kept our home form going. Another Selhurst clash against Shrewsbury on Saturday gave us the chance to get back into the top half of the table and justify the bravado I was showing at school that "of course we would come back up, we are just on loan to division two boys…"

We lost 1-0 to Shrewsbury. It was dismal, and as the papers said, "Boxer Clinton McKenzie, introduced to the crowd before the game, had more punch than Palace". His son, Leon, would play for us in the next decade. We missed lots of chances, then Phil Bates blasted home from close range from a corner and we were now looking over our shoulders at the bottom three, and not towards the top half. "I just can't get enough" from Depeche Mode was coming out of the PA as we left. Despite everything over the last eighteen months I still felt that way about Palace. However, headlines like "More woe for Dario" meant few others felt the same.

We were desperately missing a quality striker; Walsh had a poor game and Langley was looking very average. Gradi had contacted Derby about getting legendary seventies striker Dave Swindlehurst back. The difference between him and our current strikers was akin to a five-star holiday in the sunny Caribbean and a wet weekend in Luton. To my massive disappointment, after days of opening the sports pages praying for positive news, it became apparent Derby wanted £500,000 and that was way above our budget particularly as our crowds were dropping. I used to read the newspapers and Ceefax feverishly hoping we could somehow still strike a deal with Derby.

Worryingly, Gradi said he "wouldn't know where to find a striker if he had £200,000" Dario didn't sound a manager awash with ideas then! On the plus side he had realised we needed to pick up points away from home – well, yes Dario we have none so far so that would be good!

We managed that in our first game in October despite the absence of Wicks with a back injury, which left Cannon and Gilbert together at Leicester. This emphasised that the transfer fee on Wicks could surely have been better spent elsewhere. We drew 1-1 conceding a late equaliser from Lineker which had more than a hint of handball about it. The game also saw the first start for Billy Hughes up front. Hells bells, I thought Langley and Walsh were poor. We remained just below mid-table and got to enjoy the action on ITV's Big Match.

We then went had a couple of very good weeks. Firstly, we came from behind after Jim Cannon had scored an own goal to beat Rotherham 3-1, then backed that up with an away (yes, away!) win at struggling Wrexham. We were up to 7th now, and glory-be above QPR! The club had also appointed Graham Drew as lottery manager to oversee ways to "get as much money into the club as possible". This involved walking the streets asking people what kind of games they wanted on lottery cards, I was not too sure this would raise enough to get Swindlehurst back.

Just as life was looking rosier, some worrying news. Terry Venables was intending to sue Palace for "a substantial amount of money". Luckily, we had Ron Noades fighting our corner and making counter claims and the story seemed to peter out. It did little to ease the strong anti-QPR feeling amongst the Palace crowd.

Up next was Derby at home who of course had Dave Swindlehurst up front. Taking a wild stab in the dark guess what happened? Yes, right first time! He scored the only goal with a looping header in front of the Holmesdale in the 8th minute. We were poor, Hughes was dreadful up front, and Langley missed numerous chances but was unlucky when one goal was harshly ruled out for offside. Our bout of optimism was over, and we were back in mid table. Some friends had caught the action on Match of the Day and wasted no time in reminding me of it.

We saw the introduction of Steve Leahy, who looked about as effective as Hughes, in a 2-0 win over Doncaster in the League cup to progress 2-1 on aggregate. The news of the day was Palace making Kevin Mabbutt their new signing for £200,000, a sharp striker from Bristol City which meant any dreams of Swindlehurst returning were surely over. So, Dario had come up with an idea after all. He made his debut, along with a lightweight looking midfielder Steve Galliers signed for £70,000 from Wimbledon, at David Pleat's Luton. Mabbutt was isolated up front and we lost to a Moss penalty. Galliers did little to show why anyone thought he would make any difference.

We then played Blackburn at home. It was a very poor performance, with Tommy Langley living "on borrowed time" according to Gradi who also admitted "you could never see us scoring in the second half".

It sounded like Dario had lost heart and so did the club. He was promptly sacked as manager due to poor results and falling crowds and replaced by popular former player Steve Kember. He was introduced to the crowd before a 1-1 draw in a friendly against Brighton, arranged as a game at Grimsby was off due to international call-ups. It was not clear who all these internationals were.

After an event free draw at Oldham, we then won two home games to lift the gloom and to give Steve Kember a new manager bounce. The first was a fortunate 2-1 win over Norwich which saw our defence looking shaky throughout. Our first goal came when Steve Walford's clearance hit Mabbutt on the back, the ball swerved, hit the bar, and dribbled over the line! The following week against struggling Bolton we were better, on a wet and cold day we deserved the luck when Paul Jones fired in an own goal from the edge of the penalty area for us to win it. Not bad as we were missing Wicks, Gilbert, Walsh, and Hinshelwood. We were up to 11th.

We lost at Barnsley then faced WBA in the League cup, who had the formidable Cyril Regis up front. He scored twice as they beat us 3-1 at Selhurst. The first was very lucky, a miscued a shot which looped over Barron. After the game Kember said "We were not direct enough, that's why I want to buy a striker – but I'm not allowed to". Not too cheerful behind the scenes then.

There had been talk of Swindlehurst returning again, but we could not afford a £200,000 down payment with debts of £350,000 and money still being lost. We had also been linked with Gordon Davies who went on to be a great success at Fulham, and veteran Frank Worthington. The chances of further new signings seemed remote when Noades again emphasised the dire state of the clubs' finances. The kit man had to take a pay cut, the debt at the end of the season was forecast at £1.3m, crowds were continuing to fall now to below 9,000, and Noades said players may need to be sold rather than recruited. The weather was also awful over Christmas with four matches postponed hitting our cashflow.

With this air of gloom, we faced a January trip to non-league Enfield in the FA Cup in poor conditions. What could possibly go wrong? For once, not much! We won 3-2 with Hilaire, now given greater licence to attack under Kember than he had under Gradi, getting a couple and then saying, "I think things have taken off for me and Palace". It was a banana skin avoided; we were ripe for an upset, but an experienced team had done the business in grinding out a win that Enfield boss Eddie McClusky indicated we were fortunate to get. Oh well!

Further transfer speculation saw keeper Paul Barron linked with the dreaded QPR; many fans wouldn't have cried too much at his departure, but I always thought he was decent. A view that raised many an eyebrow in the smoky buffet room at East Croydon station.

After over a month without a league game we were back in action against Jack Charlton's Sheffield Wednesday. Well action was a tad generous. We lost 2-1 in front of only 8,000. The good news was the welcome return of Hinshelwood for the lumbering Bason, but despite Wicks putting us ahead Wednesday got stronger and were comfortable winners with Boulter suffering plenty of stick from the crowd. It was now Kember whose job was being questioned. To add to the joylessness, we had the horrendous Lester Shapter as referee who was intent on breaking the game up as much as possible to make it even more frustrating than it already was. There was then little entertainment at Cambridge in a dull goalless draw.

In early 1982 a few ground improvements took place, including a new Strikers restaurant, some bigger lounges, two executive boxes and a new press room. Ron Noades had received some criticism from those who felt the team should be the priority, but he pointed out that the interest free loans for these projects were only available for these expenses which were completed in the hope that the income from them would eventually help our poor financial position. A cup run would help those finances, and a 1-0 win against Bolton with a very dodgy early penalty for an alleged hand ball gave us a win. Wow, we are in the last 16 of the FA Cup and the crowd nearly got to 10,000.

More legal matters hit the papers. Palace were set to sue ex-chairman Ray Bloye relating to the £1.9 million deal that Sainsburys struck that decimated the old Whitehorse Lane end of the ground which left us with an unsightly tiny terrace and the remains of a worksite. It seems £630,000 had gone astray and the HMRC were investigating the VAT treatment. Bloye later insisted he had no liability.

We then "welcomed" QPR to Selhurst for the return of Terry Venables and the plethora of ex Palace players he had taken with him. My very good QPR supporting school friend, Andy Hamilton, made the game too and I was desperate that we didn't lose. We didn't. The game in a heated atmosphere was dull and ended 0-0 with Cannon and Wicks in commanding form at the back meaning me, my Dad, Mick, and Graham went home satisfied with a point. Wicks' performance was apparently encouraging QPR to try and take him back to Loftus Road, we didn't have many quality players and I didn't want to lose him.

The following week we lost to a last-minute goal at Charlton despite playing our part in a lively game. The winner had come after Murphy was sent off for calling the linesman "a cheating bastard." Kember was unhappy saying as it was in the heat of battle it should have been ignored. I was very concerned about relegation now being just a point clear of the bottom three. School friends were quick to remind me of this "On loan to Div two Si? Yeah, Div three next!"

A good school friend Des Jacobs came along to Charlton and enjoyed it so much he came the following week to see us draw 0-0 in the 5th round of the cup against Orient. They included ex Palace midfielder Barry Silkman, in front of a much bigger crowd of 14,500. It was a real battle, Orient kept it tight, and we struggled as usual to create much. We could have lost it when Henry Hughton (more on him later) had an effort brilliantly saved by Barron. A replay at Brisbane Road certainly put the odds in their favour and defeat in that may even hasten the departure of Wicks, who with Cannon is giving us a very solid central defensive pairing.

Before the replay was the draw for the F.A.Cup quarter finals on radio two at Monday lunchtime. So, I took my radio into school and was desperate for us be at home. Andy Hamilton's QPR were also in the draw so he came with me to a quiet spot near Hazelwick School's tennis courts and we listened with bated breath. Guess what? In the third match out we drew each other and on their dreaded plastic pitch. That would be a big, big match IF we could beat Orient away. Andy Hamilton looked smug.

Tommy Langley was back in favour for the replay at Orient, replacing Walsh to partner Mabbutt up front. It was a scrappy game but glory be we nicked it with Smillie, who has had a poor season, getting the winner with a cracking volley from Langley's lay off after Ian Moores had thankfully missed a penalty for them. We then got a point at Orient in an atmosphere-less Sunday lunchtime league game.

For reasons that I cannot recall we then played IFK Gothenburg in a friendly. Playing a full-strength team we lost 3-1. With a vital league run-in not to mention a big Quarter Final coming up it was a curious interlude in front of just over 1,200.

Meanwhile there was a big meeting at Solihull which debated some of the problems in the game. These included boring matches, the frustrating offside trap, possibility of summer football to raise crowds, the perilous financial state of many clubs such as Bristol City, and the much frowned upon professional foul. From memory no brilliant plan was devised to cope with these issues despite Jimmy Hill and Matt Busby being involved.

Palace were in the transfer news. Struggling striker Ian Walsh moved to Swansea in exchange for the lively winger David Giles. Meanwhile once again my hopes were raised that Swindlehurst could return, the club submitting a six figure offer despite the financial woes. Noades considered that a striker could score the goals that may bring some of the crowd back even indicating this could lead to us being promotion contenders next season which did seem a little optimistic. This may be funded by somehow offloading the slow ineffective Brian Bason to Portsmouth, and for a larger fee Neil Smillie to Luton.

We then travelled to in-form Rotherham, managed by Emlyn Hughes, who had won seven in a row so welcomed our struggling team with open arms. Even more so once Barron dropped a cross to gift them a goal, and Cannon missed a penalty. Kember admitted "we gave it away." We were now just one place above the relegation zone albeit with games in hand.

All would be forgiven if we could win next week though. It was the FA Cup Quarter Final at QPR, who had three supporters in my class at school. In the last eighteen months I had been the victim of much piss-taking as we suffered disaster after disaster. I was desperate that we won this match. Even teachers were saying "good luck tomorrow" to me on the Friday. That evening I barely slept, crikey, if we won we would be in an FA Cup Semi Final at a big ground with a massive crowd and wouldn't I enjoy walking into school on Monday.

The thoughts of this after our dire recent past were almost too exciting to be true.

QPR were 7th on the fringe of the promotion chase. We were a place above the bottom three. They were playing on their plastic pitch too that gave them such an advantage. They seemed to have many of our better players from last season plus Venables. But come on Palace let's do this, somehow, I prayed.

My Dad had managed to get seats in the upper tier in Row C behind the goal at Loftus Road and we were joined by Graham and Mick. The crowd was packed in on all four sides and I remember "Seven Tears" by the Goombay Dance Band and "Saddle up" from David Christie being played twice before the game as the bitter feeling between the clubs rose leading up to kick off. I had a stress headache building already as the players left the pitch following the warm-up.

In this atmosphere of extreme tension the first half was tight. Cannon was surprisingly playing in midfield but added some grit, and Gilbert and particularly Wicks were solid at the back. Rangers had the better of the first half with Stainrod threatening throughout. Our full back David Boulter had his finest hour with a vital goal line clearance, but we offered little and it was 0-0 at half time. If it stayed that way it would a hell of a replay at Selhurst under the lights. The second half was much the same on the bouncy plastic. Watches were being checked when QPR got a corner with four minutes left. The ball fell for Clive Allen, who turned neatly and fired in the winner. I was devastated and hardly spoke for the rest of the weekend. Loftus Road went loopy. Allen ran up the other end apparently to goad the Palace fans. I had my head in my hands for the rest of the game and that was it. Dream over, no exciting replay and instead just a relegation battle to endure. I walked into school on Monday and much to my surprise everyone was very decent. I expected QPR scarves hanging everywhere around my desk, but Andy Hamilton understood how I felt and was very generous. Allen meanwhile was investigated for his gestures after scoring. He apparently wanted to tell the Palace fans they were winning 1-0. We were already aware of that. Allen was later cleared of blame for his antics, and just warned about his future conduct. 6th March 1982 is a date that has stuck in my memory ever since, the thump in the guts I felt when that goal went in has never been forgotten.

Three days later we had a vital league game against Cardiff who were a place below us so in the relegation zone. In front of a paltry 6,500 freezing souls, we won with a second half goal by Langley. The programme the following week showed a fabulous picture of him celebrating the winner in front of a deserted old stand "lapping up the applause". Earlier Cannon had missed another penalty and the crowd were getting on the players' backs. The club sold the original programme from the postponed game in December, costs clearly outweighing the benefit of producing a new one. Money was also saved by only turning on the floodlights in full as the players were coming out for night games.

The on-off-on-off Swindlehurst deal was off again. Derby having rejected a £150,000 deal of which Noades, and his deputy Bishop, were prepared to pay the deposit personally. Kember was furious and said the board could "get on with it if they didn't realise you had to pay the money for good players". It'll be interesting to see if he lasts in his caretaker role very long.

Kember was equally as forthcoming on his concerns after we lost 4-1 at Derby "I don't see too many problems on the field. It is the uncertainty off the field that is causing all the problems. There is talent on the books, there are no problems of honesty and moral, but everybody is confused and upset about the uncertainty". Chants of "Noades out" had rung round the Baseball Ground at regular intervals. Meanwhile Liverpool, who we were being touted to topple two years ago and become the team of the eighties, won yet another trophy by beating Tottenham in the League cup final.

We then faced a trip to Chelsea. My Dad and I sat in a near deserted and decaying West Stand. Indeed, the whole area around the ground was grim with lots of rubble about. We were staggered when Mabbutt and Murphy put us two up by half time. Of course the Chelsea onslaught came after they pulled one back, but we clung on and it was a very valuable three points. Worryingly it was reported Jim Cannon had been transfer listed. It had been a tough season for him as the arrival of Wicks meant he was shoved about between full back, midfield, and defence as he was so competent in all of those. We surely couldn't do without him.

That result, and news of a constructive meeting between the directors and Kember largely stopped a supporter protest group before the game against Luton covered by the Big Match on ITV. The first half was a classic, amazingly 2-2 after fifteen minutes – after all we were OK at the back and but not OK scoring goals! Despite us leading twice Luton got a third before half time but a fine strike from Smillie got us a point against a team who would get promoted at the end of the season.

The team at this stage needed Cannon in midfield. We had a lack of bite in there with Murphy, Giles, Smillie and Hilaire. Mabbutt was looking lively up front but had only scored 4 in 16 league starts so it was still clear where the problems were, particularly as Langley had managed just two in the league all season – and it was now mid-March! The defence had been sound, unsurprisingly with Wicks, Gilbert, Cannon and Hinshelwood. Boulter struggled at times but was still young. Did we have enough to stay up? It would be tight.

Next up was Leicester at home, Boulter struggled against their lively front line including Lynex and Lineker and we lost 2-0. Had it not been for the impressive Wicks and Gilbert it would have been way worse. Kember's job was again under threat and he admitted after the game that "Leicester seemed to want to win and we didn't". It was reported that Gerry Francis was being approached to replace him.

Bad news followed. Steve Wicks signed for QPR on deadline day for around £300,000. This represented a loss of £357,000 for his fourteen games for one of the most expensive centre backs in Europe last summer. There was nearly an exchange taking Barron to QPR too, with Burridge coming back to Palace which would have been very popular but sadly that fell through. The money from Wicks was absolutely necessary. The financial situation was so bad that the sale was required for us to get through next season with debts including £160,000 to the HMRC, and to cover liabilities entered into when we had income based on being in the first division and crowds at least three times as high. There was speculation of another boardroom upheaval, but it seems any prospective new owners were put off by the dire financial situation.

A couple of dour away games followed. A 1-0 loss at Blackburn when we should have had a late penalty for a foul on Langley, and 0-0 at Newcastle with Cannon restored to centre back.

It was then reported that Steve Kember had been given a three-year contract.

We played Grimsby as we moved into April. They were bottom of the league and a win could see us open a gap between ourselves and the relegation zone. We lost 3-0 and were shocking, the lumbering Bason was back, the crowd was only 7,500, there were slow hand claps and many verbal attacks on Ron Noades. I ended the game sat on the Arthur Wait terrace in the weak spring sunshine with Des feeling very fed up as we were only two points above the bottom three and looked such a desperate team.

Our optimism wasn't heightened as the next game was at high flying Watford who were full of pace and strength with the likes of John Barnes and Luther Blissett. However amazingly we pinched a draw at Vicarage Road with David Giles getting our goal. Barron made a string of saves until Watford got a 76th minute equaliser. A valuable and unexpected point.

We couldn't build on it on Easter Monday though, a terrible performance losing 1-0 to Chelsea with Steve Lovell getting barracked by the crowd for an inept display. The guy who sat in the seats behind the enclosure would yell "wake your ideas up Lovell" relentlessly whenever he was on the pitch. He usually had a point, but it made Dad and I laugh. It was the best crowd of the season,17,178, but only because there was a healthy Chelsea contingent to watch us fall into the relegation zone that we had been flirting with all season. The crowd were not happy with Price and Brooks struggling in midfield and with only Mabbutt up front we looked punchless yet again which raised tensions and led to some crowd trouble. My mood was not helped when Steve Kember pointed out that we wouldn't be in such peril if "we had done better in our last two home games (which we lost)". Indeed Steve!

The following week we hosted Oldham. The only change from Chelsea was Price out and the lightweight Galliers in. However, we certainly needed to show the character Kember was calling for before the game. An early goal from Hilaire, playing closer to Mabbutt than he had against Chelsea, gave us a boost and then we ran out easy winners 4 (yes 4!!!) -0 and led to Jim Cannon praising the confidence of the team and assuring fans we wouldn't go down and didn't sound like a player likely to leave. On the platform at Norwood Junction the mood was way better than it had been the previous week.

We then faced two away games. The Hilaire and Mabbutt combination struck again to give us three vital points at Grimsby and then a gritty point at Bolton made it a great week with seven points gained and no goals conceded. Great work and showing the character Kember had demanded. Instead of going to Bolton, Des, I, and two other school friends Paul

Harris and Mark Farrow went to cheer on whoever Brighton were playing – turned out to Manchester United who won.

During this promising week Palace picked up striker Paul Wilkins, released earlier in the season by Spurs, plus there was talk of a club take-over by property developer Graham Martin that never came to anything.

Another rearranged evening match because of the Christmas postponements completed our April, this time home to promotion chasing Watford. This was the first evening game I went to on my own and if I thought we would make a game of it I was wrong. Watford gave us a footballing lesson and were everything we were not – quick, athletic, agile, and strong and beat us 3-0. Although we were not the best of sides that performance remains one of the most impressive from visiting teams I have seen at Selhurst. It was no surprise that they took the first division by storm and got to a cup final two years later.

Next up were Barnsley, with former Palace favourite Ian Evans in their line-up. Despite leading through Mabbutt, we again struggled, Lovell had moved into midfield but didn't "wake his ideas up", and we ended up losing 2-1. We then lost at Shrewsbury raising the relegation heart rate once more.

To much relief Mabbutt scored the winner at fellow strugglers Cardiff which meant if we could beat Wrexham on the following Tuesday, we would be safe.

I was very tense and prayed it didn't all to come down to our final match against Newcastle. Surprisingly, Wilkins got a start and played alongside Mabbutt. Even more surprisingly to the fella behind us, Lovell "woke his ideas up" and had a storming game. We were two up at half time both scored by the 18-year-old Wilkins. This was despite no-nonsense Gilbert going off with an injury and being replaced by lightweight Galliers after only ten minutes which caused me great anxiety. This was relieved by my goal celebrations so ferocious that they seemed to shock those around me. Didn't everyone realise how big this game was! Obviously, it didn't end stress free. A harsh penalty was given for an alleged foul by Cannon on their big striker Ian Edwards and the disappointing crowd for such an important game had a stressful last fifteen minutes. Edwards was later sent off for a fracas with Cannon, luckily big Jim didn't incur the wrath of referee Axcell. We had won and were safe. Thank god for that.

We finished losing 2-1 to Newcastle which saw the debut of Gavin Nebbeling a South African centre back.

We finished 15th, and four points outside the relegation zone.

I produced an average mark out of ten league table for our players. The top three were Steve Wicks, David Giles and Billy Gilbert, and the worst three David Price, David Boulter and Shaun Brooks.

There was a post season friendly played at East Grinstead. We won 7-1 and Mike Elwiss (an excellent striker for us five years previously) played for us and scored a hattrick. Be good if he returned I thought. He didn't.

The last game at Selhurst was England's 1966 world cup team (mainly) playing a Charity eleven which included Alan Mullery which Des and Des's Dad took me to. A light-hearted way to finish the season watching Mullers get plenty of stick!

Chapter 2: Season 1982/83 – The arrival of an old enemy.

Steve Kember had taken the manager's job midway through the previous season. His positive influence in midfield for Terry Venables brilliant young team a few years ago meant he had some popularity with the fans. It certainly hadn't been plain sailing, but it seemed very likely he would be given this season to see if results could be improved despite a budget of pretty much zero.

Alan Mullery had been at Charlton the previous season and was considered the enemy at Selhurst. He had insulted Palace fans at a heated 1976 FA Cup second replay when managing his Brighton team, who became bitter rivals, against us.

So, let's play the theme tune from a popular TV show at the time. Tales of the Unexpected. Guess what? Palace sacked Kember and chairman Noades replaced him with the oh so obvious choice....Mullery! He was to be assisted by Ken Shellito. Mullery had been approached by no less than Benfica during the summer, and even after being appointed at Selhurst was offered the Portuguese job.

There were also some incoming players. The bulky striker Ian Edwards, who had a fracas with Jim Cannon last season, joined as did full back Gary Williams, and tough tackling midfielder Henry Hughton. All on free transfers. The arrival of Hughton gave the possibility of Cannon reverting to centre back as Hughton was certainly capable of providing the bite in midfield that could otherwise be missing.

Edwards scored a neat header against Wimbledon in the one season wonder League Trophy. This seemed to be some glorified structure for local pre-season friendlies, not that we progressed far. We drew at Brentford and were thrashed 3-0 by Millwall with former Palace midfielder Chatterton scoring, and playing against future Palace characters Trevor Aylott and Sam Allardyce. Happily, we beat Brighton in a friendly which is never a bad thing.

Mullery got a mixed reception to put it generously when we opened the season proper at home to Barnsley. He steered clear of his previous insults to Palace fans and links to our bitterest rivals by reminding us we still had five of the squad that did so well under Terry Venables. He hoped to increase competition for places either with young players coming through or further signings, ideally another centre back.

The team played well. Hughton and Murphy excellent in midfield with contrasting styles and Cannon and Gilbert as reliable as ever at the back, but the other new signing Williams looked weak and nervous. We had, against the run of play, gone behind but Hilaire – back from a spell with the San Jose Earthquakes – got a richly deserved equaliser. Despite this promising display, I was happy with a point as once Murphy went off, we struggled – he was certainly living up to his "Zico Murphy" crowd nickname. The downturn may have been down to Lovell who still had not "woken his ideas up" from last season.

Football in general was struggling. There were fewer people watching on TV, falling crowds, many dilapidated stadiums, hooliganism, and many thought the game dull. It was a million miles away from the revolution that took place ten years later after Gazza's tears at the 1990 World Cup. I disagreed with the negativity and had no understanding of why people didn't enjoy it! I thought tales of what other kids in my school did at weekends were dire. Highlights for them included a thrilling trip to McDonalds in Crawley.

Our second league game was at Rotherham and I was soon in a bad mood with LBC reporting that we were two down in ten minutes. Hinshelwood pulled one back and then luckily Mullery must have read my mind as had brought Edwards on and he combined with Mabbutt with the later making it an archbishop and a second point.

After two draws which way would the season go? We had two home games coming up and a chance to make a good start to the season for the first time in three years.

The crowd for the first, against Shrewsbury, was only 6,578 which was partly due to many staying away because of Mullery's appointment. His arrival was emphasised by Kember reportedly threatening to sue the club. The ground started to feel very big with banks of empty black seats, plus big gaps on the Holmesdale terrace despite the Whitehorse end still in development.

My friend Des joined my Dad and I and we saw a very solid performance as we beat the Shrews 2-1. Hilaire and Mabbutt were both excellent and the team, including the previously struggling Williams, looked sharp.

This was followed by a 2-0 win with the same scorers against Blackburn. Des had encouraged another friend, Paul Harris, to come along and he also got to enjoy Hilaire tearing Rovers apart and laughing at the bizarre officiating of Mr Burden. Even the crowd was up by 1,000 and we were 6th!

It was looking good under Mullery, like him, or as many still did, loathe him.

Another positive night followed at Portsmouth where good old Steve Lovell got an equaliser on the night and we got through to the second round of the League cup on aggregate. Meanwhile Paul Hinshelwood moved into the top ten in the Palace all time appearances list, I caddied for him at Ifield Golf Club at a pro-am and he was a very decent bloke.

I tried in the coming days to convince my Dad that after a long working week in London it would be a good idea to go to Carlisle on Saturday. Inexplicably he wasn't so keen. Poskett scored four goals in a 4-1 defeat. It would have been a long journey home.

During the week England drew 2-2 in Denmark. Tricky to see how this relates to Palace but it did. There was crowd trouble which resulted in a £50,000 shirt sponsorship deal for Palace getting cancelled as the company did not want to be associated with football. Ron Noades was an angry man as with gates needing to increase by at least 3,000 to break even losing this income was bad news.

The sports reputation was that bad and even as a supporter you could be generalised as being "one of those football hooligans."

Gloom was brushed aside as Graham and Mick joined Dad and I to see Palace thrash Middlesbrough 3-0. Mabbutt is looking the business up front and I was delighted to see Edwards score at home having been very impressed with him.

Despite the finances still being in a perilous state, and the negativity around Mullery's appointment, we were back to 6th which was way better than last year. I was hopeful that we could have a very good season with certainly no relegation worries. I even dreamt of being in the promotion race.

Next up were those bitter rivals QPR. Memories of the devastating cup defeat were still in mind. It was nothing like the game last March, a dull 0-0 in front of less than half of the FA Cup crowd. That was followed by a 1-0 loss at Bolton with reports saying, "it is hard to see how they got themselves into the top six." We were better at Burnley the following week, a lively game which we led at half time but a mistake by Williams and a late winner conceded meant we were now back in mid-table.

We weren't brilliant against Oldham but won 1-0. It was a memorable as incredibly our keeper Paul Barron nearly scored twice. First a long punt caught the strong wind and hit the post before being scrambled away, the second was another huge kick that Andy Goram pushed around the other post. Mabbutt, whose brother Gary made his debut for England in the week, did get the vital late goal.

The crowd, a sparse 6,600, was another financial worry. The depths of winter hadn't even arrived yet although October had been very wet. These dwindling numbers were depressing as we had made a decent start to the season. It was thought to be down to Mullery's controversial appointment, and he rarely even had an article in the programme. However, I was pleased we had an experienced manager, instead of some of the recent appointments such as Walley, Gradi and Kember. I knew Mullery could produce a good team in this league and just may be shrewd enough turn us around. If he could hopefully the crowds would return, as TV revenue was minimal. I just tried to draw a line under his past shenanigans.

His shrewdness didn't help at damp Newcastle, a Waddle goal after Keegan's side-step resulting in a 1-0 defeat. A couple of weeks ago the Geordies faced Fulham and reports said, "there was no chance of Palace copying the thrashing Fulham inflicted." We had Fulham next up in the league, that worried me!

Well, look at us! Unbeaten at home at the end of October! An improved crowd of 15,000 saw why Fulham were third in a highly entertaining 1-1 draw. In truth they should have won playing a slick passing game. Happily, Hilaire nicked an equaliser in a game played in a good spirit typified with Fulham boss Malcolm MacDonald smoking a cigar alongside Mullery in the closing stages.

There had recently been a new ruling that the much-despised professional foul would result in a red card, I didn't like that and thought it would be way more exciting if a penalty was given or a straight run at goal from the halfway line.

We went to Stamford Bridge next, where Micky Droy committed a professional foul with a deliberate handball to stop Mabbutt racing through on goal. A yellow card was given. I was not impressed. Hughton was again very useful in midfield and Barron made some excellent saves to make sure we remained safely in midtable with a 0-0 draw.

We had overcome Peterborough in the second round of the League cup, and we drew Sheffield Wednesday in the third. They looked like a top of the table team as Megson and Bannister took two close range goals very well right in front of Dad, Des, and I on a breezy Holmesdale Terrace.

Leeds and their crowd, which had been causing some trouble across the country, arrived at Selhurst in fifth but Mabbutt got his ninth goal of the season following a scramble from a corner. My Uncle Mick took a dim view of the equaliser when Terry Connor turned sharply in the box and let out a bellowing "Noooooooo". Still unbeaten at home though.

Meanwhile Jerry Murphy was attracting interest from Chelsea, and surprise surprise QPR. With such a thin squad we could do without losing him but when West Ham, second in the first division, were linked as well it become more worrying – unless we got Brooking in exchange my Dad said!

The following week my Dad and I went on the official Palace supporters train to Leicester. Des came too but booked on the Inter-City and met us there. On a grey day in the dingy small, covered terrace there were a group of noisier supporters that Des and I edged towards hoping we could get a draw particularly after Cannon went off injured at half-time. We didn't get that draw. We got a win! A fine run and cross from Hilaire being nudged in by Mabbutt. We held on despite the threat of Lineker which left the legendary Palace fan Joyce "the voice" in fine spirts. It had been an exciting game and we were up to tenth.

When I met Des again in London, I talked to him about next season, and even if my Dad couldn't go, or after working in London all week, didn't want to, we would be a year older and should travel to away games together. There were worries about the level of hooliganism, but I disregarded that. I thought what a great way to see the country and those football grounds that had been just words in newspapers and my scrapbooks up to now and taking advantage of cheap club trains. After all we had enjoyed a top day out. He was certainly up for it, so next season we planned to go to lots of away games. Nothing could stop us in my eyes.

The following week saw promotion chasing Wolves come to Selhurst. My Dad and I were joined by Des and Graham and saw the debut of new signing Chris Jones. I remembered Jones as he scored a few when Spurs rattled up a cricket score against Bristol Rovers a few years previously, and with Edwards and Langley injured it seemed a good acquisition on a free from Manchester City. We made a dazzling start with Cannon heading us ahead, then our new signing ran through and rattled in a second. Wow, two up in the first five minutes! Too much too soon? Matthews and Clark got the impressive Wolves level. Then with half time cups of tea plus Mars and Yorkie bars being looked forward to Scotsman Andy Gray scored a typical header and we went in behind. "Two up but behind by half time, that really is the pits." said Des. Great entertainment though for Match of the Day. I was happier when Hinshelwood equalised from about the HP sauce isle in Sainsburys, but was left distraught when Wolves got a fourth, and our unbeaten home record was broken. They deserved it though and had an excellent team. Gray in particularly was way too good for this league, our old favourite John Burridge was still a class keeper, plus John Humphrey who set up the winner and would have a big part to play at Selhurst in the future. With Culture Club's "Do you really want to hurt me" coming out of the dodgy PA system we made our way home.

There was nothing positive about our next game. A 4-1 thrashing at Grimsby meant that successive defeats left us seven places off the bottom. Worries were eased as we got revenge over fourth placed Sheffield Wednesday following the cup defeat to get back to mid table with a 2-0 win. It was a committed performance with a flu ridden Barron replaced by Fry in goal and Edwards and Mabbutt both injured leaving what was to become the "legendary" Jones and Langley combination up front. Our efforts were emphasised when Hilaire raced back to tackle Andy McCulloch who was through on goal. Sadly, McCulloch didn't spend the rest of his time away from Selhurst. The board were happy with Mullery's efforts in guiding us to midtable and he was invited to join the board of directors, surely this year there would be no relegation trauma at the end of the season.

The programme this season was a rectangular one. The cover had finally changed from Vince Hilaire having a dribble in front of a deserted Arthur Wait stand to one from the Fulham home match which showed Ray Lewington, a future Palace coach and joint manager, clutching the far post. A further change was on the PA, long-standing and popular John Henty being replaced by Spike Hill who was fine. But I just associated Henty's voice with more successful days on the pitch.

Paul Barron was again missing in goal, but the Sunday Express reported Palace were "full of ideas, power and commitment" as Langley scored his third in three games to get us a point at bottom of the league Derby. The bad news was Kevin Mabbutt getting injured and facing months out - not good news as he is easily our best striker. This was promptly followed by Paul Barron's sale to WBA for £60,000. He was often heavily criticised by others but not by me and I was very disappointed. Long serving reserve David Fry would replace him in goal. It seemed less certain that Barron had been flu ridden.

With this gloomy Christmas news, we faced Charlton on 27 December who included star striker Allan Simonsen, but it was Chris Jones who stunned many with an excellent header to get us a point.

The next day my Dad and I made the two-hour coach trip to Cambridge. No players moaned about tiredness despite two games in two days! We saw Cannon score a second half own goal. I was unimpressed with Cambridge; they couldn't even spell our players names correctly in the programme.

We completed the double over Leicester on New Year's Day 1983 with Langley finishing off some quick thinking from Hilaire at a free kick.

During the week Noades took out a long-term loan to pay off some safety costs and was mooting an idea of selling shares in the club to raise money for Mullery to improve the squad. These shares were to be sold in units of £100 each, more than a season ticket which made it seem unlikely that there would be sufficient demand to have us heading the queue for a stack of quality signings.

I spent some time figuring out some 1982 statistics showing our top scorer was easily Kevin Mabbutt, with Vince Hilaire winning my vote as man of the match most often.

On 3 January 1983 Rotherham took an early lead at Selhurst when Fry did little to raise fans confidence in him when a miskick went under his dive. Hilaire then went down in the box and we got a second half penalty. "That dive would have done Brian Phelps proud" whined their manager Emlyn Hughes. I didn't care when Hinshelwood tucked it away. In the programme articles from Mullery became more regular and he was stressing the need to turn draws to wins if we were to challenge for promotion. Sounds a good idea!

We played York City in the FA Cup third round at Selhurst. Mullery had already said we expected to go through, and we did, with Fry looking more confident in goal. Nevertheless, Mullery did bring in keeper John Phillips and full back Gary Locke, from Chelsea, on loan.

The league position got more worrying after we lost 3-1 at Barnsley. Then a result that hurt a lot more, a comprehensive 3-0 home defeat to QPR with Venables having four ex Palace players in the line-up and arch enemy number one Clive Allen getting the first two. They also frustratingly played a relentless offside trap that we lacked the guile to breakdown. The relations between the two clubs declined even more as Rangers chairman Gregory and Noades had a legal tussle over amounts due following Venables move. The matter even ended up at the high court.

We played first division Birmingham in the FA Cup and Dad, Des, Graham, Mick, and I all stood on the Holmesdale terrace and watched David Fry have an excellent game making numerous saves particularly when Hinshelwood, who had been unusually struggling this season, was getting out paced at right back. We took the lead just after half time with a brave header from Edwards. We knew it would be tough to hold on and even more so when Hughton was sent off for a lunging challenge on Mark Dennis who had been known to produce plenty of these in his time. Maybe lucky for Henry that he was sent off! Hold on we did but there was some bad press when a steward lunged at rugged Brum defender Noel Blake.

The fifth round saw us draw Burnley at home, a winnable game as they were one off bottom in our league and unbelievably for such a struggling team, we had the chance of consecutive Cup F.A. Cup Quarter Finals.

Des and I were continuing our discussions at school of going to most away games next season. We decided to go even if the worst came to the worst and we went down. The excitement of that was building plus the feeling of growing up a little. Those plans were to be wrecked when my Dad came home with the earth-shattering news that we wouldn't even be in the country next season as he had been offered the chance to work in Ottawa for a year. The family consensus was we should go, and we would leave in mid-August. The prospect of all this gave me sleepless nights. How about school? How about missing family and friends? Mainly how about Palace!! I told Des, "Blimey mate that's a long way to come every Saturday". He was very disappointed but promised to keep me up to date with the sagas of Selhurst.

The following week Dad and I enjoyed another trip on the Palace special train, this time to Shrewsbury taking just under 3 hours and costing only £7. Once again it was an excellent day out and we got a decent draw. I took a dim view of the Sunday paper reports which said we had to survive "heavy" pressure. I thought we looked the more likely to score throughout the game.

We watched us draw 0-0 with Burnley in the cup, a disappointing result. Many thought the highlight was an overweight fan who appeared no stranger to a pub running on and "scoring". It was as close as we got, particularly with Chris Jones misfiring up front. A replay would be tough, we all knew that.

After that we outplayed Bolton and won 3-0 with Ian Edwards dominating veteran centre back Mick Doyle. He offered much more than Jones or Langley against a team with future Palace signing Neil Redfearn. The crowd was shocking though, just 4,496 and very disappointing as we had been just about hitting our breakeven target of 10,000. We followed that by losing at Oldham to two first half goals and continuing to show our ability to miss the chances we create even including a fifth minute penalty "We will have a new penalty taker now Paul Hinshelwood has missed four this season". promised Mullery.

So, to the replay at Burnley and the chance to reach the quarter finals again. Des and I spent many a fun evening playing snooker in his parents' garage and we found the game was going to have live radio commentary. So, we played a few frames listening to a tense first half. Still 0-0. Could a second replay be on the cards, maybe at Selhurst we hoped. The second half followed a similar pattern as we spent less time potting balls and more time standing by the radio willing a Palace goal or full time. Then with nine minutes left disaster. Penalty to Burnley. Gutted. The commentator described Mike Phelan stepping up to take it…."and he's put it wide". Cue mayhem in Des's garage with much shouting and joy as we raced round the table with high fives until in the midst of it we heard the dreaded words "…will be retaken." After the heartbreak of the QPR game last year we suffered again as Trevor Steven put the second effort away and that was it. "That really is the pits." said Des. It was indeed. Mullery called the whole penalty affair "shocking and disgraceful so typical of our luck this season".

There was more bad finishing on show when we were beaten by Newcastle, it was back to Jones and Langley so unsurprisingly we didn't trouble the scorers and Varadi and Waddle won it for them with some ease. Like this stage last season, we were clear of the bottom three but only just. I thought the chances of survival had increased when Palace signed experienced 6-foot striker Ally Brown from WBA. I was soon to find out that I was being a tad optimistic on the effect Mr Brown would have on our team. Meanwhile David Price, who hadn't featured all season, left to join Orient. I was pleased when we signed him a couple of years ago, but he had been very disappointing albeit in a declining team.

Dad, Des, and I made our way to third place Fulham aware that we were in for a tough game. There was a big Palace crowd on the big open terrace behind the goal with a wind blowing off the Thames to our left. Just before half time their impressive centre back Roger Brown rose to head a winner in front of us. Our strike pairing of the slightly more promising Ally Brown and less impressive Jones did little to indicate we would equalise.

We rather cheekily put the prices up 50p for the home game with Chelsea, as we expected a good number of their fans to be heading to Selhurst. The crowd was only 13,479 and a dull 0-0 meant it was even worse value for money. Again, Jones and Brown were ineffective, and it was left to Cannon and Fry to ensure we got a draw. Another key player in our point was my former much loathed referee Lester Shapter but, glory be, he did us a favour by somehow not giving Chelsea a penalty when Nebbeling hauled down the constantly dangerous Cannoville. Mullery was admitting that the team were getting nervy now. We were just 2 points off the relegation zone, and he said we were "second best throughout". I won't miss playing Chelsea, the "one man and his dog" song when on relentlessly.

The season had started so promisingly but it was now looking like another dogfight to stay up. Des had started supporting us in the bad times that's for sure, and I wanted him to see that supporting Palace isn't always like this as my Dad and I knew very well.

Jerry Murphy was given the penalty responsibility and he stepped up at Leeds to give us the lead at half-time. Des and I had gone to cheer on Aston Villa at Brighton (0-0) and took turns clutching a little radio to hear three bits of dire news. Firstly, they equalised. Secondly Murphy had his second penalty saved by veteran David Harvey. Thirdly, Leeds scored a last-minute penalty and we had lost and were now only outside the relegation zone on goal difference.

We drew 0-0 against Cambridge and I thought how much we missed Edwards and particularly Mabbutt who may be fit for the vital trip to Charlton next week.

It didn't start well at the Valley with Carl Harris putting them ahead after Derek Hales shot was blocked. Surprisingly we levelled, Hilaire crossed, and Brown efficiently put it away. This had a very strange effect on me, as I stood up to cheer, I had a severe shooting pain go from my neck into my head, it was very nasty, and I felt quite faint too. Dad took me to the St

Johns ambulance to check me out, I was deemed OK but still had a thumping headache. Our joy of an equaliser didn't last as Steve White put them ahead again after 25 minutes. The rest of the game was dull but there was mass hysteria in the Palace end when Kevin Mabbutt came on as sub and immediately looked a threat, but frustratingly we couldn't get an equaliser. We are now one-off bottom, our worst league position since our third division days.

The following week we played Carlisle; we needed a win big time. Strangely during the week, I had a bout of optimism and wrote into the Palace postbag programme feature and said how I thought we were set up for promotion next season. I had disregarded the slight issue of being threatened with relegation this season. This letter was later spotted by good friend Dave Lewis who has since taken much delight in mocking my prediction.

That threat of relegation looked worse when Alan Shoulder put Carlisle ahead in front of a paltry 5,675 at Selhurst. It was a low moment. Luckily, we got an own goal to get us level and then Ally Brown with a header from Murphy's cross made it 2-1 to take us out of the relegation zone on goal difference. "I didn't have any fingernails left at the end" said Mullery. The small Whitehorse terrace, otherwise known as "the Sainsburys", was now open and schoolchildren were given free admission. Some thought they must have been very badly behaved during the week to have that stressful afternoon imposed on them.

During the week I should have been working towards my CSE exams, but I was more pre-occupied with how we could get a result at Blackburn. Not to mention hoping we would win the short-lived Evening Standard five a side, but we lost to Brentford in the semi-finals.

We got thrashed at Blackburn and it was reported that there was an air of resignation about our fate and the team got a tongue lashing from Mullery. To make matters worse that weekend our old rivals Brighton won their F.A Cup semi-final. Meanwhile Ron Noades was threatening to sack players if we did go down and pay rises for others would be scrapped "It would set us back three years" he said. There were still many teams involved in the battle to stay up, including Chelsea close to the relegation zone with David Speedie saying players there had lost interest. Noades saw the same problem at Palace.

We had to beat Grimsby at Selhurst and with a few school friends joining us we did thanks to Hilaire and Brooks scoring second half goals in front of 5,909. The following day I started training with a weekend team that these friends played in. I was a bit nervous as I was being encouraged to come along as they wanted me to play in goal but the current goalkeeper, Cameron, didn't know. I did feel awkward, and Cameron ended up playing for someone else. I had a little more understanding on how difficult it must be when you join any football club.

Dad and I went to Wolves the following week on the £4.50 supporters train. We had been there in 1979 when we were near the top of the first division and saw Andy Gray sign for them on the pitch. He scored the only goal of the game today. We stood in the away end, high on the corner and I didn't think Wolves looked that good considering they were just about guaranteed promotion. "They'll come straight back down" I said. Maybe a hint of bitterness in our defeat.

I spent the Sunday writing out the fixtures all teams at the bottom had left to figure out how many points each would get. It did little but make me even more stressed about staying up.

May began with a critical home game against Derby. We produced a cracking performance to win 4-1, Kevin Mabbutt showing why he got the reception he did at Charlton with two well taken goals. He is just head and shoulders above our other strikers. Before the game my cousin Graham wrote to the club to get me a PA dedication before my season off next year. Some further joy spread around Selhurst with the news that Brighton had been relegated so if we stayed up we would play them next season. "That's a big one" I told Des.

Ron Noades admitted some mistakes in the Sun on 10 May. Firstly, in sacking Malcolm Allison, and in paying £657,000 for Steve Wicks. He has also been looking at ways to trim the staff should we get relegated.

We were up against Malcolm Allison in our penultimate away game of the season at Middlesbrough. Des and I decided on a snooker session with LBC on. We were one down at half time. Then LBC told us "there is a penalty at Middlesbrough…". Come on we thought please be for us "…for the home team". Obviously, they scored and we were on a relegation tightrope. Jack Boulder, the Daily Mail reporter, cheered me up as he had Palace down for an unlikely win at 6th placed Sheffield Wednesday next week. If that happened then Mullery's confident statement that "we won't go down, don't worry" would be justified for sure.

It was an exciting game at Hillsborough, the highlight being Jerry Murphy's chipped goal, but it mattered little as they had already scored twice. Luckily, Rotherham didn't win at Leeds which meant if we avoided defeat in our last game at home to Burnley we would stay up.

So much for hoping for a stress-free finish to the season! Mullery was violently sick during the night before Burnley with the tension of it all.

The papers produced a who's up and down list, for division 2 it said "Relegated - Bolton, Rotherham and Burnley or Palace". I didn't like that so crossed "or Palace" out in my scrapbook.

So, with my Dad, Des, Mick, and Graham, I made my way to Selhurst on 17 May 1983 for the deciding match. It had been only 4 years since we beat Burnley to get into the first division, now we needed a draw to stay in the second. I was pleased with the team chosen as we had our best two forwards Mabbutt and Edwards starting. A massive crowd for those times of 22,714 showed up, well over double the average and the Holmesdale terrace that we were on was packed for once and even the programmes sold out. Burnley could stay up if they won, so it was never going to be easy. I told Des this is how the atmosphere always used to be.

The first half was tense, with Palace having the edge. Edwards missed a chance from close range early in the second half, but as tension rose Hilaire darted down the wing and squared and Edwards bundled it over the line in front of the newly completed Sainsbury's terrace. Burnley pushed forward after that, but we were worthy winners and had survived. But we had seen ourselves even closer to relegation than last season when we sacked two managers.

We finished 3 points above the relegation zone, in 15th again.

I had been so optimistic before Christmas. It seemed Mullery's experience was working but Mabbutt getting injured and signings not being very successful makes my programme letter predicting a promotion push in 83/84 look very unrealistic.

This result was promptly followed by the signing of experienced keeper George Wood from Arsenal. I had always rated him and was very pleased. We gave Chris Jones a free transfer which was no surprise. Despite struggling this season it was sad to see Paul Hinshelwood also given a free, one of the five remaining from our glory-days of a few years ago. I certainly didn't agree with letting Ian Edwards go, his size made him a handful and a good foil for Mabbutt. However, with four non-prolific strikers Jones, Langley, Edwards, and Brown we needed a clear out to hopefully free wages for new signings.

I went through my marks out of ten for players during the season, Murphy coming out on top with Hilaire second and

Barron and Gilbert tied third. The lowest average mark when to Lovell followed by Langley and Hinshelwood.

On the way home we talked about next season. The division would be tough with Manchester City coming down, and we would have two games against Brighton to enjoy.

Then I realised I wouldn't be here to see it….the bitter winter of Ottawa beckoned.

Chapter 3: 1983/84 - News from afar

The thought that I would only attend three matches in a season seemed incomprehensible six months ago, but that was the unwelcome reality I faced.

We left for Canada, as my Dad had a secondment, for a year. At first it seemed like a holiday. The weather was warm and sunny, and we were in the very plush Park Lane Ottawa hotel, before we eventually moved to a very comfortable house. I used the hotel notepaper for my Dad and I to make predictions for the season ahead, neither of us had Palace going up. My memories of this season are mainly second hand through regular letters from my cousin Graham and good friend Des plus reports from the Croydon Advertiser which we arranged to have posted over every week. No websites or email in those days.

"It'll be a wonderful experience" the world and his wife told me. I thought I would much rather have the experience of going to Barnsley, Carlisle, and Cardiff etc over the next year! It wasn't that I was against going, I knew it was a once in a lifetime opportunity and be good for my Dad's career. However, as the season drew closer I felt very sad that I would miss the first season of Palace travel Des and I had been planning. This was something we discussed during many games of tennis before watching the 1983 Cricket World Cup.

During the summer Palace were interested in Spurs veteran Steve Perryman with Palace Chairman Noades saying "He's the type of midfield general we are looking for." Spurs were not impressed and accused us of making an illegal approach. I liked the idea of our link with Joe Jordan as well, he may be getting on but would surely be a handful in the second division. More controversial was the former Brighton captain Brian Horton, coming from our bitterest rivals he would do well to win any fans over. Finally, Aston Villa's championship winning midfielder Dennis Mortimer was a possible signing. None of these got close to materialising.

Instead, we signed the experienced defenders John Lacy and Les Strong from Fulham. They were joined by striker Andy McCulloch from Sheffield Wednesday for £5,000 plus £1,000 for the first 15 games. He had scored 23 goals for them last season so that seemed very promising. We also got Stan Cummins who had a good reputation as a nippy forward from Sunderland and happily cost nothing. Again, Mullery was dealing on a near zero budget as the club had made a loss of £223,000 in the previous year.

A couple of departures, keeper David Fry to Gillingham and striker Tommy Langley to AEK Athens for £5,000. The Langley fee was open to doubt as AEK said they paid £130,000. Not true said Noades.

There would be some live league action to enjoy on TV this season, 10 matches of the newly sponsored Cannon League for which clubs would receive £2,000-£10,000. It didn't seem likely that these games would be shown in Canada!

A pre-season French tour which involved some crowd trouble in Calais was followed by defeat to the Japanese National team which Des and I attended with about 1,300 others together with a 1-1 draw with Southampton, and a 2-1 defeat to QPR. These unencouraging friendlies came at a big cost. Our best striker Kevin Mabbutt suffered a knee injury and will be out for three months. He was replaced promptly by striker John Fashanu on a short loan from Norwich. We won at Wimbledon to complete our pre-season, during which Fashanu got injured too so we then acquired forward Tony Evans from Birmingham. The merry go round continued with Ally Brown leaving for Walsall which to me was no great loss.

In the Ottawa sunshine I frantically tried to find a newspaper shop to find the result of our first game, against Manchester City. I was crestfallen to read that we had lost 2-0 with new signing Lacy having a poor game. Strangely there was no barrier between the supporters in the old stand and the pitch for this opener.

Palace nearly overcame injury problems, plus terrible traffic delays arriving just nine minutes before kick-off, to draw at Shrewsbury with McLaren's 25-yard strike equalising Cummins excellent curling freekick past young Steve Ogrizovic in goal. This was followed by another Cummins goal at Huddersfield, who fought back to win 2-1, with little Cummins then being sent off so another player was now missing. Stan was at least getting good reviews from Graham and Des.

I was now starting school in Ottawa. I was used to walking into class in a school I knew well and having long chats with the others about the weekend's results. It was therefore very difficult walking into Lisgar school with nobody to have the usual lively banter with. It was a big imposing building where I felt very uncomfortable and homesick. I found out which classroom I was in by finding my name amongst the seemingly never-ending sheets of A4 on the wall. But I had no idea where the classroom I was allocated to was, I asked a teacher who just said, "can't you just follow the signs". I felt unwelcome and lonely. I remember the feeling of dread when the hotel lift reached the ground floor on a school day very vividly. I couldn't face going after a week and moved to Colonel By High School. I hoped there would be someone there who at least knew who Crystal Palace were, or even Liverpool come to that.

Mullery couldn't believe the club's luck when we lost another player to injury, this time full back Gary Locke in the Sunday home draw with Fulham. John Fashanu came on as sub, and Mullery said "He played well, and his parent club Norwich are keen for us to take him". We didn't despite agreeing a £15,000 fee. He went on to play for England. The England youth midfielder, Gary Stebbing, made his debut at 17 to highlight our injury and suspension crisis.

Mullery was furious at a "disgusting performance" as we lost the second leg of a League cup tie 3-0 at Peterborough. We had won the first leg 3-0 but lost the tie on penalties, with future England keeper David Seaman saving from Murphy and Cummins. Mullers threatened to fine the players, which provoked Players Union Chief Gordon Taylor to dismiss that idea as farcical complaining that "fines are being thrown around like confetti." The win bonus from the first leg was donated to a children's party instead and Mullery issued an apology to fans in the next programme. His words with the team had little impact as we lost 3-1 at Newcastle, and Gilbert to suspension, after he kicked out at Wharton.

Far more positively we were somehow able to bring back Peter Nicholas, a tough tackling quality midfielder who had played a key role in our glorious rise back to the first division in 1979. That would be certainly tick the box of a midfield general and was a coup at £150,000 which seemed a fortune to us then. We also didn't need to pay until next summer so had the chance to rummage behind a few sofas whilst Noades was busy approaching local companies for donations!

We were bottom of the league. That depressed me almost as much as hearing how bad we could expect the Canadian winter to be. The thickness of the coats and boots in the town centre were giving me some indication. I had changed schools by now and many kids were very unfriendly which didn't help, one saying I only counted as half a person when asked if anyone was in class. There was one guy, Craig, who did have an interest in UK football and certainly knew who Palace were, so we did chat a bit and I felt I at least had one friend.

During some dark days in September 1983 for both me and Palace it was great to receive some updates from Graham and Des by post. I used to read them at least twice to make sure I didn't miss any important bits of news, particularly about Palace.

Des was particularly scathing at this time "Palace are not worth letter space, they are bottom of the league and lost 3-0 at Peterborough – yes, Peterborough!" Graham had sent over some newspapers reports on a succession of dire Palace performances.

Our injuries meant we were surprisingly able to call off the Cardiff home game, but then got a much-needed win beating Portsmouth 2-1 with Paul Wilkins getting a rare but welcome game and scoring the first.

My school days got better in October. I was now only there in the mornings but it was still, as a shy sixteen-year-old, something I found very difficult. My Mum used to give me a shot of Cherry Brandy some mornings to "give me a boost". Colonel By played the national anthem every morning just to remind me, as if I needed it, that I was away from home. I would have died for that to be replaced with "Glad All Over" one morning! After school my Mum and I usually went out for a lovely lunch somewhere which was always the day's highlight. In the afternoons I would work on some correspondence courses so well organised by my Dad and Crawley's Hazelwick School then watch Minder and Bob Barkers Price is Right on TV.

Palace got better in October with a great away win, 3-1 at high flying Middlesbrough which Mullery described as "Bloody marvellous". I didn't see that coming. Our missing players list was so bad that Murphy was named on the bench despite being unable to play.

We backed that up with another away win, this time at Cambridge going two up before surviving a second half onslaught. Then Tony Evans scored his third in two games at the end to clinch the points and get us close to mid-table. The lift these two wins gave me were very valuable and gave me a spring in my step at Colonel By. Also, injuries were improving, and Palace struck one of these new-fangled shirt sponsorship deals with Red Rose superstores so some small plusses at last.

In this era it seemed impossible for us to maintain any momentum. We lost to a late goal to Derby, at Grimsby despite Nicholas making his welcome reappearance, and at home to Barnsley in front of 6,233. We did get a 1-1 draw at Leeds in the first game of November, but even that had frustration as we seemed to have scored a perfectly good second goal which was deemed to be offside. Two departures followed, Shaun Brooks moved to Orient on a free presumably as we had signed Nicholas, and coach Ken Shellito for personal reasons.

We finally managed our first league clean sheet of the season beating Cardiff 1-0 in front of an even lower 5,299, with the returning Jerry Murphy coming off the bench to get a late winner. Injuries were becoming the bane of this season, and a 2-1 win against Oldham was achieved at the cost of losing Cannon. Nicholas had been crocked playing for Wales in the week and Noades was most dissatisfied over lack of compensation from the Welsh FA. He threatened to ban Nicholas from playing international football which obviously didn't go down well. "Its bloody crazy, if this is his view, I am very disappointed in him," said Peter.

The following week we had a trip to promotion chasing Chelsea, which I trudged about in feet of Canadian snow feeling very pessimistic about. I could just about pick up on the BBC World Service that we were staggeringly two up in half an hour including one from former blue Gary Locke. Sadly, Hollins got one back before half time and after Speedie equalised it took some gutsy defending, with Gilbert as sweeper, to get a valuable point.

I was starting to work out which matches I could get to when we went back to England for about ten days at Christmas. It was looking like the Brighton and Charlton games on consecutive days, then Shrewsbury at home. With endless days of -10 or colder temperatures I daydreamed of this quite a bit. So much so that one dull day walking to school after the latest blizzard I got completely lost as path's had been totally covered in even deeper snow. Once I made it home, frozen, I read Palace had completed nine new heated executive boxes. For £200 eight could watch the game with a three-course lunch thrown in. That sounds warm I thought.

The one person I could chat happily to at school was very valuable, Craig was the only friendly face! We were talking on route to our next class when he said, "I'll miss our chats, but we are moving permanently to Vancouver over Christmas". I must have given him a look that said you have no idea how much I will miss them.

We reached our highest league position this season when we beat Sheffield Wednesday with a Giles goal. He was also getting improved reviews from Graham and Des. I was disappointed Mullery didn't get manager of the month after going through November unbeaten and even beat the winner, Jack Charlton, at Sheffield Wednesday.

With this run of form I was hoping we could get a win at bottom of the table Swansea, but again we couldn't maintain a good run losing 1-0. Injuries were building yet again to the point that we had to field two apprentices the next week at home to Carlisle, Dave Lindsay and Wayne Martin, plus 17-year-old was Stebbing in the starting eleven whilst striker McCulloch was so ill he was sick on the side of the pitch. Despite that we played well but lost to two late goals. Injuries were so bad Palace put reserve keeper, John Phillips on alert, as it seemed reliable goalie George Wood may be required to play up front! Meanwhile this week the striker we got rid of, Ally Brown, scored the winner for Walsall against Arsenal in the League cup.

The programme Graham sent me was talking about the Christmas games, that made me feel very excited as I would be at Selhurst in a couple of weeks now. That excitement was not lessened by a weak first half performance that angered Mullery in a 2-1 defeat at Blackburn.

At long last we were on our way home for Christmas, staying in Hastings. I knew we had to return to Ottawa, but I was determined to just enjoy the time we had at home and not just dread returning to the endless snow. Well, that was the plan anyway!

My first game back was on Boxing Day, home to Brighton, a match with a hostile atmosphere. Mullery described it as a "tradition of friendly rivalry" I wasn't absolutely sure on the friendly bit. Graham and I were given a lift to Crawley by Mick where we met Des and his Dad and off we went to the game which was not quite what I had daydreamt about. Veteran ex Manchester City keeper Joe Corrigan made two excellent first half saves from McCulloch and Hilaire, then Brighton upped their game and won 2-0 with Wood letting a weak shot from Palace reject Smillie, of all people, dribble past him. Particularly in these times if it could go wrong it would.

The next day Des, Graham and I went to Charlton for a near replica of last season's frustration. We were losing when on comes Mabbutt the messiah back from injury with us trailing 1-0. But we still can't find an equaliser. If we had it would have been pandemonium in the packed away end, and I would have had a great memory to take back to Canada instead of watching our worst spell for nearly 30 years. It was made worse by losing to a team containing Chris Jones. I despair!

I at least got a goal against Shrewsbury on New Year's Eve with Stebbing scoring. We held out for a while thanks to Wood in goal, but despite Lacy who got a stack of stick from the crowd. This was harsh as the fella played on with a painful broken nose for much of the game. It was no surprise when Shrewsbury equalised.

Now back to Canada where forecast temperatures were dipping to -23. I spent some time on my return producing statistics for the 1983 calendar year which showed Vince Hilaire made most appearances and be only a goal behind top scorer Tony Evans who had managed six. Our home record was decent, but we had just two away wins in the year. There was little else to do to pass the time, even a five-minute walk could be painful in Ottawa's biting winter so producing these depressing statistics had some benefit.

Palace would have been relieved the Cardiff away game on the 2 January 1984 called off with injuries yet again piling up. Meanwhile an un-named second division team had bid £100,000 for Billy Gilbert, but he had just been given an award for our player of the first half of the season so I was pleased it was not accepted.

Palace faced Leicester in the third round of the FA Cup. City had got promoted last year despite Palace doing the double over them. With eight minutes to go a massive punt up field from Wood nearly caught out City keeper Wallington who tipped the ball over the bar and waved an acknowledgement at Wood. However, glory be, we scored from the resulting corner with a Gilbert header to win 1-0.

We tried to ease our striker issues by approaching Swansea for veteran Bob Latchford, but his wage demands were too high, and that idea was promptly scrapped. Our 3-1 defeat at Manchester City means we had only gained one point and scored four goals in seven league games.

I used to hear the Palace results in Canada by a weekly Saturday morning (Ottawa time) phone call between my Mum and my Gran, who I was very close to and who knew all too well how desperate I was to hear of a good result. If Palace had lost then it would be a very quiet subdued "Hello" and the early conversation would be in a tentative hushed tone similar to that used by a dentist giving news of root canal treatment.

The inevitable bad result was eventually given. I had fully expected this on 21 January as Palace faced high flying Newcastle. I listened as my Gran answered our call with a very cheery "Hello love, they won, they won 3-1, did you hear Palace won 3-1." I could hear the joy making its way over the Atlantic, and it was so much in need as the winter dragged on and on and on and on……Any event that made any of my Mum, Dad, and I happy for a bit was good news for us all.

In view of my one friend leaving at Christmas I felt the best bet to engage with the other kids was to try and learn more about the sport they talked most about, Ice Hockey. I watched a match one weekend in full and tried to make sure I had a couple of points to make if I could raise the confidence for a chat about it at school. Monday morning came, the daily national anthem was played, then the group behind were talking about the game I watched. Here goes I thought "I see what you mean about Gretski, he is pretty amazing." The reply of "What do you know about it" was the final straw. I spent the next lesson in the toilets thinking things over and eventually concluded that if they don't want to engage with me then I won't bother with them and I'll just the tick the days off until May when the school year finished. That approach made life easier and took the stress away of even trying to make any friends. All this made the hope of a cheery call from Gran on Saturdays even more important.

I wished I was home for the FA Cup fourth round clash with West Ham. A massive crowd of 27,590 showed up at Selhurst and it would have been great to see the ground bursting at the seams again. After an hour of fiddling about with my radio and a plethora of coat hangers hanging off it to boost the reception, I could finally pick up some distant Palace commentary on the BBC World Service with Saturday Special hosted by Paddy Feeny. As I stood by my bedroom window looking at the latest blizzard I heard a report of a massive scramble, did he say McCulloch had scored? I could barely hear "Yes, 1-0 to the second division team". Wow! How long to go? Oh, over an hour! Commentary switched between our game and Portsmouth v Southampton where Peter Jones was commentating, I was hoping he would keep quiet about our game but then the dreaded "There is further news at Selhurst Park and its real Roy of the Rovers stuff." was uttered. What did that mean? Another goal for the plucky Palace? Then George Hamilton reported that Swindlehurst (obviously!) had levelled with a diving header during another scramble. At the final whistle I put the local Ottawa radio station CFGO for some music with a tinge of anti-climax and Irene Cara's "What a feeling" came on. It would have been had we won, but it was an impressive result though against an excellent West Ham team fourth in the first division with Brooking, Lampard, Stewart, and Cottee in the line-up. We lost a one-sided replay 2-0.

If that was thought to be the highlight of the season, you'd be wrong. The following week a more low-key match with Middlesbrough attracted 5,819 and we won 1-0. But that's not the whole story! In the 48th minute we had two players sent off, top striker Mabbutt for a second booking and player of the season so far, Gilbert, for foul language in protest. The rest of the team were furious, as were the crowd. Palace then produced a tremendous performance and when Hilaire was brought down Nicholas put the penalty away, and with magnificent defending we got three vital points.

Our injuries were finally easing, with just Stan Cummins a long-term absentee. It had been so bad that manager Mullery had to play the second half of a reserve match to make the numbers up.

This easing of injury problems helped us to get useful draws at Fulham and Barnsley with late equalisers in both to keep us seven points clear of the relegation zone. We picked up five bookings at Barnsley which annoyed the club so much that they wrote to the Football League saying many were unfair. We couldn't build on these results though and defeat at home to Grimsby meant we were still some way from safety. This game saw the debut of 18-year-old Phil Barber. He became the first member of our more successful teams to play for the first team.

We yet again didn't score at home the following week as the Leeds match ended goalless but did see the return of Cummins as sub. Out of 92 teams we are 90th in terms of home goalscoring throughout the football league. No wonder crowds are so disappointing with the team also just a place outside the relegation zone.

Barber scored his first goal for Palace at Oldham, but we lost 3-2 despite equalising twice. Our injury jinx struck again when striker Evans managed to get injured in the warm-up. Our position wasn't helped by a 0-0 home draw with Huddersfield. Hells bells still no goals being scored at home, no wonder just 5,000 showed up. The loyal souls haven't seen a goal for three home games and were putting pressure on the club to buy our way out of trouble. But Noades made it clear he was doing his best to keep us away from a winding up order and his number one priority was to keep the club afloat. Derby were in an even worse financial mess and the fear was they would go bust, but if their results were cancelled we would be in even more relegation trouble, not that I was being selfish….

At long last some proper joy on a Saturday morning with news of a first half goal from Evans to give us the lead at Portsmouth who had been in good form. Regular World Service reports said we were holding on with Nicholas outstanding in midfield and Cannon marking Mark Hateley superbly. After a few scares we did get three points to give us all a welcome lift.

Having failed to loan Mel Eves and Wayne Clark from Wolves we faced Cambridge at home, who scored after a minute. With our dire goalscoring ability at home it sounded bleak. We did equalise but our domination of the rest of the game deserved more. We were worse at fellow strugglers Derby losing 3-0 leaving Mullery furious "I am disgusted, I will make them train harder. At half-time they didn't deserve a rest, so I sent them out to wait for Derby."

With the team struggling and crowds falling it wasn't the best time for a testimonial but Selhurst hosted one for Paul Hinshelwood as a Palace Past and Present team beat QPR, who included Clive Allen, 4-1. Meanwhile Noades launched the Palace Club, benefits for a £5 fee were to include cheaper admission and away travel and wait for it....priority booking for cup finals – well it's a matter of time surely!

A very large Chelsea contingent meant that we broke the 20,000 barrier on 14 April, and we did well with Lacy getting good reports from Des and Graham which was rare. Despite that a late Nevin goal meant we lost again. Graham thought Chelsea would be "cannon fodder" in the first division. The programme cover changed to players standing with club shop produce on the Holmesdale terrace. They were as spaced out as the crowd were most weeks.

To help our ailing strike force Kevin Mabbutt played in a reserve match this week so will hopefully be available for the tense run-in as we try again to avoid relegation.

We got our fourth away win at Cardiff with an own goal and a strike from Cummins which put us seven points clear of the relegation zone. George Wood did the business too with a penalty save. That gap was reduced to just four when we were well beaten at old rivals Brighton to make it just one point out of the last four games against them. Eric Young got their third, we would meet again in a few years.

This reduced gap gave me plenty of stress leading to the Charlton home game on 23 April, and it was a nervy phone call back home. My Gran picked up the phone, what would the tone of her voice be I wondered "Hello loves" I heard in a bright and bubbly tone. We had won 2-0, with goals from sub Mabbutt and Cannon. We were getting close to safety now.

That was so useful as we faced a trip to top of the table Sheffield Wednesday the following week which we lost to a dubious Mel Sterland penalty which sealed their place in the first division. Mullery was happy despite the loss "We were playing against the referee and 27,000. The team is the best I have here and it showed".

That team was Wood, Lock, Hughton, Murphy, Cannon, Gilbert, Mabbutt, Cummins, McCulloch, Nicholas, and Hilaire.

We finally eased the stress, at least for another season, with a comfortable 2-0 over Swansea with Cannon and Mabbutt scoring before half time. Cannon wasn't fit, but injuries to Locke and Gilbert led to him insist on playing, Mullery was delighted "What more can you want, he did us proud." I was left thinking he, and the others from our glorious spell a few seasons ago, must find it tough playing what was an important game in front of just 5,318. The final two games saw us come back from two down to draw at Carlisle then a 2-0 defeat to Blackburn.

This meant we finished the season two places and five points ahead of the relegation zone. The top scorer, Tony Evans, with seven was given a free transfer. I would doubt many top scorers in a season have never scored at home. Les Strong, unimpressive as an over-the-hill full back was also released as was injury ridden Gary Williams.

I produced a graph showing our fluctuating position in the league. We never got to the top half. I produced several league tables based various criteria trying to find one where we were in the top half. Finally, success, our defending had us at a heady 9th. There was also a programme league, this would have been impossible without the help of Graham and his friend Richard who had kindly air mailed many to me.

On my last day at the school, I just said goodbye to the friendly Biology teacher and at the end of the path turned back and looked over my shoulder for the last time at the building.

Thank god for that I thought. Eventually life improved in Canada largely as my Mum, Dad and I stuck together so well, a holiday to Toronto and Florida, spring finally came, and we had visitors including Graham and my Gran. The season had been difficult to follow from afar, and it was sad to be disconnected from Palace. I knew no matter where or when our first game was played next season, I would be there. I wouldn't care if we lost 10-0 I would enjoy it.

I played Duran Duran "Rio" album for the 100th time, then left the house and sneaked some large gin and tonics on the Wardair plane home. These tasted so much better than my Cherry Brandy's on freezing school mornings.

Chapter 4: 1984/85 – Ron's gamble.

As soon as I got home from Canada, Palace were on the back pages.

Alan Mullery, who had managed to keep Palace up despite a near zero budget and lingering unpopularity for his unfortunate Brighton past, had been sacked. Clearly chairman Ron Noades couldn't see any sign of improvement, but it was unexpected nevertheless. Many of our senior players were said to be upset and were considering leaving, some thought they may be finding a way to get out of a sinking ship. Mullery ended up at QPR, with Venables having left them to move on to Barcelona.

Previously Noades had used his previous Wimbledon connections to entice Dario Gradi to Selhurst, a move viewed as a disaster by many fans. This time he used the same connections to appoint the Dons current manager, Dave Bassett, who had enjoyed considerable success in the lower leagues. He vowed to bring a new playing style and was planning to speak to the players to see if they wished to stay at Palace once an end of season trip to Marbella was completed.

Bassett then suddenly changed his mind, possibly having looked at our squad and considering the minimal budget available and went back to Wimbledon. When the players returned their new manager had already resigned!

Speculation commenced on the new man for the hotseat. Keith Burkinshaw formerly at Spurs as was one, as was former flamboyant boss Malcolm Allison. However, unexpectedly Palace appointed a man to take over the club with the same financial restrictions as Mullery with no experience at all, Steve Coppell. The former England and Manchester United winger was to be assisted by popular ex-

Palace defender Ian Evans whose experience was thought to be vital to rookie Coppell.

Coppell was clearly a risky appointment. His top-notch playing career was finished by a knee injury in 1983 and he was just 28. I hoped he may bring a few out of favour Manchester United players with him, maybe Remi Moses. Coppell needed to get active in the transfer market as our top scorer last season, Evans, had been given a free transfer along with striker Wilkins and winger Giles. He started by acquiring Arsenal's reserve left back Brian Sparrow who was being kept out of the team by no less than Kenny Sansom, and Fulham striker Tony Mahony. There were two more departures from our 1979 team firstly Billy Gilbert moving to Portsmouth for £100,000 via a tribunal, then Vince Hilaire for £50,000 to Luton. Both would surely be big losses and hard to replace for that money. More positively Kevin Mabbutt agreed a new two-year deal, and we signed big striker Trevor Aylott as part of the Hilaire transfer. He had a decent goalscoring record and I was optimistic he and Mabbutt could form a useful partnership.

Peter Nicholas had become unsettled which was a worry, and our old friends QPR were sniffing around him. Gary Stebbing, despite receiving less than complementary reviews from my friend Des, had been made captain of the England Youth Team. Des thought this showed how dire the future of English football must be.

We were short at centre back following Gilbert's departure and failed in a bid for Sunderland's Gary Bennett. This was a player we would be relentlessly linked with for years. We instead signed defender Chris Whyte from Arsenal on loan, and winger Alan Irvine from Everton.

There was little sign the comings and goings had helped as in pre-season, we only beat Torquay in a West Country tour and Hapoel Tel-Aviv 3-0.

I was glad to be home after Canada. Des had met us the day we got back and wasted no time introducing me to the world of pubs by taking me to the Moonraker in Crawley which had a pool table. Let's go I said. I was a little nervous at first, and my first faux pas was to knock a pint over a regular which did little to help. The Palace world was discussed at great length.

A few days later I caught the train from Three Bridges and headed up to Selhurst for the opener against Blackburn. I could go to the game, enjoy it, and not be thinking about the cold of Canada for the first time in eighteen months. It seemed little had changed though when we went behind following a defensive blunder, but a vastly improved second half saw little Cummins grab a deserved equaliser. With Sparrow, Whyte, Irvine and Aylott all making debuts it was a decent result. I was so happy to be back, the £3.50 to stand on the enclosure seemed a bargain.

A rare 3 o'clock kick off for a League (Milk) cup first round first leg match against Northampton was dull but I still enjoyed it, I would enjoy any Palace match right now! We won with a Nicholas strike 1-0 with Trevor Aylott struggling and their beanpole, Wakely Gage, impressive at the back. Matters didn't improve for Trev during a 4-1 thrashing at Shrewsbury, he was sent off after 5 minutes! He was promptly fined by Coppell. We at least got through the cup tie at Northampton drawing the second leg 0-0. Unsurprisingly Coppell said, "It was not a classic".

We continued to look anxious in front of goal losing to a solid Birmingham team 2-0, our best openings came through Irvine but how we need Mabbutt back. I made two appearances in the programme, a letter predicting good times ahead and with Des in the photo from the Blackburn game. Cannon was back from injury, but Mahony looked unimpressive with Aylott up front so goalscoring could yet again be an issue. Despite a hefty Brummie contingent, the crowd was only 6,500.

We were at old rivals Brighton next. How a win would lift the spirits I thought as Dad, Des and I met Mick and Graham. We looked the better team, but we had nothing up front to trouble the Albion centre backs, a certain Young and O'Reilly. They brought on veteran Jimmy Case as sub, and he sparked them enough for O'Reilly to get the winner. The large Palace crowd were frustrated, and Brighton fans took great glee in finding out we were now bottom of the league "Unless we learn to take our chances we will stay at the bottom" warned Coppell.

I had restarted school at Hazelwick to take some o'levels. My Canadian qualifications were meant to be o'level equivalents but just how many prospective employers would accept that was a worry. It did feel a bit of an anti-climax as good friends had left or weren't now in the same class as me. I was still recognised as being a big Palace supporter though and the mickey taking over our league position was already rife. After last year I didn't mind at all.

I followed a Tuesday night trip to Sheffield United on Teletext. With 12 minutes gone we were losing again. I stared at the screen endlessly updating page 304 willing it to change. Then it did "Murphy 69" appeared. A point! Get in! Then gloriously "Mahony 88"!! A 2-1 win, and all the way up to the heady heights of 19th!

We produced a cracking performance at home to Leeds, at long last taking our chances to win 3-1. I met Des later in the Moonraker for drinks and many games of pool, it was winner stays on and with funds limited I made sure I got plenty of frames for my 30p. Sadly Des had lost heart with Palace a bit after last season, and with us struggling in the early games this year, which was a shame as I was hoping he'd be up for a trip to Manchester City. I had decided to go to City after the Leeds win, and I brought a club train ticket from the little portacabin behind the Old Stand. I walked back to Norwood Junction thinking how I could prevent my Mum and Dad worrying about me going on my own to Manchester next week. I lied "I met a friend at football, his name is Harry, and we are going to Manchester City next week, that's fine isn't it?" "Whose Harry?" asked my Mum looking a bit concerned "Oh, he's about 20 and has gone to lots of away games and says it's really safe. He's an estate agent." I thought an estate agent made my made-up friend sound very sensible.

Palace had some knockbacks during the week. Losing at Sunderland in the first leg of a Milk cup tie at Sunderland which saw Jim Cannon break the Palace appearance record. Then transfer moves for Brian McDermott, Andy King and ambitiously Frans Thijssen didn't work out.

My first solo away trip was up to Maine Road on 29 September 1984, the excitement made the week at school beforehand drag like hell. In the ground I saw Graham's friend Richard and it was good to have someone to chat to during the game, in a fenced off away area in the big kippax terrace. It didn't start well though, City going ahead through Gordon Smith (he who thankfully didn't score in the 1983 cup final for Brighton) after 12 minutes. Nobody expected a prompt equaliser, but we got one with a fine shot from our best summer signing, Irvine, which eventually found its way into the far corner of the net. Sadly Kinsey won it with a fine breakaway goal, but it was great to be at a big ground with a good atmosphere. I had heard stories of a local Saturday paper that all the scores in it by 5.20 which sounded too good to be true. When we got back to Manchester Piccadilly there it was, but there was a queue and our train left in five minutes. I just managed to get a copy of the "Pink" in time with a headline "City Salute for Kinsey" then sprinted onto the train with a minute to spare. As we got towards London, I noticed I was opposite a very small guy who was contorting his neck so he could read the back page. Eventually I just gave it to him to read, and he asked if I wanted a "tinny". I wasn't sure what that was but said yes anyway and it turned out to be a can of ale. Result! We chatted, then had a couple of pints in Victoria which I had to order despite being underage as he looked way too young. He was Jay Sisley, and he was a great travelling companion for years. Harry would be promptly forgotten. Jay left for his train to East Grinstead, and I got mine back to Three Bridges thinking what a good day it had been, and I was certainly keen for more of this. On the walk to platform 19 a big burly chap who looked aggressive said "Alright mate, saw you on the train" He turned out to be Conrad who said he would "sort anyone out if they had a go at a Palace fan". I felt a bit safer now too!

The usual crew of my Dad, Mick, Graham, and I were optimistic for a result at home to Barnsley, a Sunday kick off to see if that would entice a bigger crowd. I was cheerful as a favourite song at the time "Japanese Boy" by Aneka was played pre-game so I thought it would be a good day. We played well but couldn't score, and then lost to a sucker punch. "One of those games" my Dad said. That was followed by a 0-0 draw with Sunderland which saw us out of the Milk Cup, Des's view of Stebbing did not improve after that game. We then lost at Carlisle, with Noades keen to find a millionaire backer "to put the cream on the cake now I have cleared some debt". No millionaire was forthcoming, and vague links with Status Quo came to nothing.

Jay and I booked on the 11.28 supporters train to Tommy Docherty's Wolves together with his cousin Adrian. We had a good giggle on the train playing three card brag for massive bets that reached the heady heights of 5 pence at times. We saw Noades outside Molineux and Adi offered to buy him out "I've got a fiver mate?". "Uncle" Ron smiled. It was a tight game, but Wolves clearly had better players. They were two up through our top scorer last year, Evans, who obviously did score at home this time, and Melrose. Cummins scored a consolation penalty in front of only 6,656. We are now in the bottom three, and for the fourth season in a row it looks like a second division relegation battle. Oh joy.

A couple of derbies produced just a point. Alan Irvine scored a cracking 22 yarder but we drew with Fulham, a match that included a phone link to the Australian supporter's club at half time. It was disjointed and rather embarrassing though "much like Palace" Des said. The other was a 3-2 defeat at Wimbledon in front of 3,000 Palace fans despite a weird kick off time of 11.15 on a Sunday.

Palace made two signings from the non-league this week in a bid to increase the squad depth. Steve Galloway from Sutton United then Andy Gray from Dulwich Hamlet. I was disappointed it wasn't the Scottish striker Gray but in time I wouldn't have swapped our Andy for anyone. Chris Whyte's loan ended despite hopes it would turn into a £120,000 transfer and he returned to Highbury. I wasn't too bothered though, he looked good initially, but I thought we could spend that money more wisely. I was wrong - he went on to win the first division championship with Leeds in 1991.

We made it nine without a win against Shrewsbury despite going two up in twenty minutes, but shortly afterwards we had the entertainment of an outfielder in goal as Henry Hughton went between the sticks after Wood got a knee injury. It was strange that Coppell didn't know if he had volunteered, in the days before a sub keeper could be named it seemed bizarre we didn't have a plan for this scenario. It cost us when a keeping error made it 2-2 but Henry made some good saves after that to get us a point. I was furious when Stebbing was tripped in the box late on and we didn't get a penalty. Galloway looked lively coming on as sub "A striker that runs, that's a novelty," said Des. The crowd was dreadful, just 4,002.

Trevor Aylott finally scored on the 10th of November against Huddersfield, glory be! He had been getting some fearful stick from the paltry 4,927 crowd. The chant "Son of Aylott" was saved up for any hapless opposition striker who made a cock up of a chance. The shock of Trev's goal was seemingly too much for our team as well and Pugh promptly equalised to leaving Coppell to warn "If we don't stop the rot soon we'll be getting our third division gear out".

It was down to second placed Alan Ball's Pompey next, who with Gilbert at the back looked very strong. Des, Jay, and I couldn't believe it when young Phil Barber put us ahead, and just as we were thinking we could hold on Morgan equalised with 15 minutes left and we then had to survive an onslaught led by the longed haired sub Alan Biley for a valuable point. Aylott was better today, holding the ball up well. That may have encouraged Coppell to allow Andy McCulloch to move on to Aldershot on a free transfer. Nobody seemed too heartbroken at his departure, or that of John Lacy.

We now tried an 11am kick off on a Sunday against Oldham in an effort to boost crowds. Just 4,504 showed up, it didn't matter when we played, attendances were dreadful. However, my Dad, Des, Graham and Mick saw us play very well and win 3-0, our first win in 12 but we are still in the relegation zone.

Des, Jay, Adi, and I made the three-and-a-half-hour rail trip (£10.90) to Middlesbrough which involved a ride on a bus like local train which interfered with my tremendous display of not winning at brag. We met another character "Spot" on the way up. Interesting chap, who seemed obsessed with how small our bets were. There were less than a 100 in the away end and they didn't even open one stand as few locals saw us as an attraction either "no need mate, no bugger 'ere" the steward said. We were delighted with a point, and Aylott scored yet again. "He's a goal machine" said Des with just a hint of irony. When we got back to Victoria with my chest infection, Jay insisted a few pints after a fun trip would be the perfect cure. I didn't like to argue. I spent the rest of the weekend practicing brag, determined to improve. I was loving these trips despite no expectation of any good results.

One who was improving was the previously maligned Aylott, he got yet another the next week at home to Cardiff. We tried 3pm on a Sunday this time and the crowd rocketed to 6,000! Sadly, we conceded an equaliser yet again, but on a positive note Andy Gray made his debut and he was a handful. Promise there I thought. "We'll soon drag him down to our level," said Jay.

The following week Jay, Adi and I got the £8.50 club train from Kings Cross via Newark to the glamour that is Grimsby. "Wait 'till you get their mate, it stinks of fish" Conrad said. I had my doubts, it can't be that bad surely. Our tickets turned out to be in first class which was great, generally the club trains were very comfortable anyway but this was a step up for sure. Sadly, the Newark to Grimsby service was less salubrious, another train/bus contraption that crawled along. I got off and it did stink of fish. Conrad grinned at me. We walked parallel to the train line and stood in the low terrace behind the goal. Tony Ford, an ancient midfielder, looked good for them and they were more dangerous than us, but amazingly young Gray scored from Irvine's cross. A goal, and away one too, so cue mass delirium in the away end! We weren't finished there as after half time Nicholas finished a good move and we started to live the ultimate dream of a win at Grimsby. But…Wilkinson pulled one back to instil panic in our end. That was wiped away when Barber restored our two-goal lead which meant not only had we won but we could relax in the closing minutes, although Jay didn't like the premature "jingle bells" song. There were massive celebrations at the final whistle. Joyce "the voice" gave me a kiss walking out "bloody marvellous" she beamed. The journey home from Newark saw a big group of Leeds fans get on our shared train, it was great fun with lots of drinking and a loud singsong dispelling the media stereotype of all football supporters fighting with each other.

There was good news during the week as Mabbutt had recovered from his latest injury, and with Aylott in better form maybe we were on the up.

I couldn't go to the game on Boxing Day, home to Charlton. We had our traditional family get together involving pontoon and at least for me a hefty gin and tonic drinking session to enjoy. I relied on Des who went and told me the next day "We were great, Nicholas hit one from 30 yards and Barber slid the ball to Kev who put it under the keeper for our second. They got an own goal, but who cares we deserved the 2-1 win."

The trip Jay, Des, Adi, and I had to Oxford on the 29th wasn't great. The coach was perishing. The coach was slow. Where is my first-class inter-city? After well over two hours, we got out into pouring rain and a near gale and made our way on to an open terrace. Despite that the 1,000 Palace fans made a lot of noise in the downpour. Well until 11 minutes in when Bobby McDonald scored the first of five goals and we got totally outclassed. Feeling soaked we got back on to our cold coach.

I produced some 1984 statistics (a bit nerdy but hey-ho) that showed the reliable George Wood made most appearances. He was followed by Peter Nicholas who was also top scorer, that made the speculation worrying that he may be leaving.

Des and I had already booked to go to the £5.90 train to Notts County on the first day of 1985. My Dad and I went there to see a 0-0 in 1978 when Palace fans took up a certain Boney M song in relation to Vince Hilaire. New Year's Eve 1984 was my first in a pub, the Moonraker in Crawley. I got there excited early in the evening but that was dampened by the pool table being covered over. Instead, some old school friends including my old QPR mate Andy Hamilton tucked into all the different beers on offer, and as a result when I met Des at Three Bridges station in the morning I was feeling grim on the bitingly chilly and grey platform 3. "How's your head?" I asked Des "better than yours by the looks of it."

I had recovered a bit by the time we found our train which had been taken over by the club in full complete with the squeaking trolley wheeling up and down selling cut price drinks, crisps, chocolate, and sandwiches. I diligently followed Des's advice of "Eat lots to ease a hangover" and coupled with the old-fashioned individual compartments on the train giving some peace I recovered from the previous night. Well, until Spot started to enjoy his game of waking me up! The match was a struggle but thanks largely to Wood we managed a 0-0 draw and we at least stopped former Palace favourite Harkouk scoring. Feeling fine by the time we got to Victoria I was up for joining Jay and Des for a few pints in Shakespeare's.

We had drawn third division Millwall away in the F.A.Cup who were managed by former Palace midfielder George Graham, and had former Eagles Chatterton, Lovell, Fashanu and Roffey. Not my favourite venue, it was a scary place which seemed lawless with a risk of violence wherever you looked so Des, Jay and I got seat tickets which we thought would be safer. We were wrong. We walked the 20 minutes through a warzone to the old Den ground and found our seats in a ropy old stand hoping we were at least safe. We scored after 23 minutes, a header from the improving Mahony. We stood up and celebrated as normal. Then a group of massive blokes standing in the isle at the back of the stand said, "Sit down you soppy c****". We sat down. Palace were matching Millwall's commitment with Cannon and Wood excellent but just as we were thinking about a highly dodgy walk back to the station after a win, Dean Neil equalised. The boys behind us grabbed us round the neck and were jumping around celebrating, so much for segregation. Oh, brilliant I thought, they'll be at our place for a replay now.

A trip to Chelsea seemed the likely reward for the winner of the replay much to the joy of Uncle Ron "with recent weather postponements, a cash windfall at Chelsea makes this a terrific draw." We had the replay postponed twice plus the Brighton home game and Blackburn away where we had brought refundable train tickets on a trip that would have taken over four hours each way "Think of how many brag pennies you'll save," said Jay.

When the replay was finally played, who scored the winner? Go on take a wild stab in the dark. You got it, Steve Lovell had "woken his ideas up" and scored in front of the Holmesdale. It wasn't a pleasant evening. Millwall fans infiltrating the home ends and the feeling that violence was imminent all evening. In Millwall's sixth round tie at Luton there was terrible crowd trouble so maybe we got off lightly. Our retirement from the cup meant it was more likely that we would take the £150,000 on offer for Peter Nicholas who claimed the club lacked ambition "I have wanted to go since Gilbert and Hilaire left in the summer." He was a big loss when he signed for Luton.

For some reason we played West Ham at Selhurst in a friendly three days later, losing 2-1. Despite the lack of action lately with us outside the relegation zone on goal difference it seemed a massive risk as we couldn't afford any injuries and the money gleaned from a 1,542 crowd was surely scant compensation. Another obscure friendly had also been organised, this time against FK Austria in February.

Manchester City did the double over us, as they had last season, beating us 2-1 with the promising Andy Gray getting our goal. Uncle Ron now seems open to making funds available for Coppell following the departure of Nicholas, but Coppell was cautious "Everyone knows we have money, so they can sting us." We were hardly the Dallas Ewings but needed some reinforcements. Dennis Wise came along as an apprentice and played in the reserves but ended up joining Wimbledon and eventually playing for England.

I was having a busy time as we moved into February such as schoolwork, travelling to Palace games, and spending plenty of time in the Moonraker playing pool. I would try and get to the pub for opening to practice and get closer to my ambition of using the winner stays on policy to be unbeaten from 6pm to the 11pm closing. Funds were limited and I would take just £1 to the pub, that gave me two halves of Triple Crown at 35 pence each and no defeats on the 30p pool table. There was one lad who I struggled against, Lloyd, from Lymm. I resented him invading "my" table, but we became good friends and enjoyed some long pool and drinking sessions which weren't wholly conducive to school life. I even used to sneak down the Moonraker in school lunch hours with a friend Paul, once we saw a teacher in there and feared a telling off. Instead, as he walked past us he said "I haven't seen you, you haven't seen me. OK?" We nodded and I trudged back to the snow gutted to hear Palace's trip to Birmingham was off.

Having had a miserable journey to Oxford in December Dad and I were expecting little from the return at Selhurst. Coppell knew after that thrashing we needed to "play for pride". We battled very well and with eight minutes to go put together an excellent move involving the rapidly improving Gray which Aylott finished off. A great 1-0 win.

Our efforts to spend the Nicholas money were not resulting in signings, Hiene Otto, Ken McNaught, Alan Davies and Gary Brooke were all mentioned but none relished joining such a struggling club with dwindling crowds. Instead, unknown Irish defender Ken O'Doherty arrived from Dublin University. It seemed unlikely to me that this student would boost our goalscoring tally or replace powerful Welsh international Nicholas in midfield.

Jay and I went to Huddersfield on the supporters' train, again very comfortable with Gildo operating the splendid squeaking trolley trundling up the corridor. This was the only disruption to a long card session including "Play your cards right" which Spot branded boring, then wanted to play. On the way back the stewards took a flexible approach to the "no alcohol rule" much to our joy. The game was dull, we lost 2-0 and many of the 150 on the big open away terrace reckoned the half-time band gave more entertainment.

The following Saturday was a dark day. Des and I watched a Wimbledon team humiliate us 5-0 at Selhurst, our worst home result since the war. They relied on a long ball game with pacy forwards, and tough tackling midfielders that we just didn't have the athleticism or ability to match. It was only 1-0 at half-time which was a minor miracle but after that a series of crosses were met by free powerful headers into our net. Our team looked sub-standard, lacking any fight, and any vague positivity held by a few was crushed out of them. It was a soul destroying and embarrassing day which amazingly could easily have resulted in an even worse score line such was the chasm between the teams. Noades came under intense pressure with but said he wouldn't quit or sack Coppell who supported his chairman who had gambled on him "It's nothing to do with Ron, it's down to the players and me." It was an ugly afternoon and morale was at rock bottom. It was not too difficult to see why Wimbledon manager Bassett had decided we were not a good option last summer. An action group run by Chris Wright was particularly vocal with a "Noades must go campaign" but the chairman pointed out that "unless a chairman comes in with a lot of money to pay off loans nothing will change."

After that fiasco we did well at Fulham, always a good trip, getting a 2-2 draw with Gray continuing to look promising. Coppell was quick to try and dampen down the Action Groups demonstration "They have the club at heart, but it won't help the lads on it. Civil war here won't help." Jay and I had a few drinks at Victoria and reflected that the thrashing last week may just have made us realise how much we needed to improve.

We made a step towards improving by signing Derby midfielder Kevin Taylor for £15,000. He came on as sub in a dull 0-0 at home to Wolves. We then beat Carlisle, 2-1 but only 4,330 showed up with Barber scoring twice in the opening five minutes before we spent 85 minutes hanging on. There remained considerable unrest with the leader of the Palace Action Group being ejected and threatened with a life ban.

Jay and I went on the club train to Barnsley which we shared with some good lads from Fulham who were at Huddersfield. They were happier than us on the way home having got a draw whilst we lost 3-1. I took a right gamble by ordering a "Meat & tata" pie to enjoy on a massive open terrace populated by about 200 hardy souls. I had no idea what "tata" was. Oh, it's just potato then. It took us a while to work out where the toilets were, eventually a steward pointed towards them, turned out to be a concrete wall with no roof or running water. Lovely.

As I was still at school I needed a way to supplement my income to go to Palace away games, plus the few drinks which were becoming a critical part of the day. I was entering many pool tournaments in Sussex and up to London and it was paying well. One at Shakespeare's in Victoria carried a first prize of £80 and I went up there with Dave, a bouncer, and for the price of a couple of beers he said he would help me make sure I got back if I won the prize. I duly did, picked up the money and Dave said, "Get your cue and run, train goes in 3 minutes and I don't think you're a popular winner". We legged it over the concourse and hopped on the train back to Three Bridges. That'll be another three away games paid for!

We signed the man mountain Micky Droy from Chelsea on a free in the week, and he was described by Coppell as "A big man for a big job." Droy was so big we needed to have special kits made for him. It seemed worth it though when he scored on his debut against Sheffield United, but we lost 3-1.

The disinterest being shown in Palace was emphasised on the following Tuesday when we played our bitterest rivals Brighton. The crowd was only just over 8,000 with a large contingent from "them". Aylott put us ahead, but the second half did not go well. Firstly on 66 minutes came an infamous incident. Brighton midfielder Gerry Ryan was subject of a "robust" challenge from Henry Hughton who missed the ball and caught Ryan's left leg so badly that the bone crack could be heard in the stands. Referee Milford sent him off. We were down to ten men, but so were they as their sub had already been used! We couldn't hold on and it finished 1-1. Brighton were furious with captain Wilson demanding Hughton be "banned for life". Palace fans used the "Gerry Ryan walks on crutches chant" around the country for years.

Despite Henry's suspension we should have won at Charlton. Aylott scored yet again (wow, that's 8!) and Gray could have won two penalties, and he hit the underside of the bar, but annoying Curbishley equalised late on. We got an important win over fellow strugglers Notts County in front of 4,744 with Jim Cannon keeping his record of a goal every season he's played. New signing Taylor looked steady and Droy and Cannon were proving a determined and very physical barrier at the back. This put us seven points clear of the relegation zone.

Meanwhile Marler Estates were interesting in buying Chelsea's decaying Stamford Bridge, and then Selhurst Park for £2m. Noades believed Marler's intention was to find somewhere for Chelsea to play so their site could be used for development, or possibly to enhance Chelsea's ground then have Palace play there and build offices or houses at Selhurst. "They do not care about Palace, they just want to find a dumping ground for Chelsea" warned Uncle Ron who has his critics but was no mug.

Jay and I travelled to Leeds on the club inter-city the following week and were joined by the team on the way home, but they had got stuffed 4-1. I missed my first match of 1985 on the following Tuesday, a 3-0 defeat at Birmingham. Instead, I followed the game via teletext and some gloomy reports on LBC.

With Palace now pretty much safe I missed another game, a 2-1 win over Portsmouth to play tennis with Lloyd and then go on a pool and drinking session in Brighton. I was starting to get into trouble at home during these binges as I had a habit of losing my front door key. At about 4am I would bang on the door and a bleary-eyed Dad would come down the stairs to let me in. For some unknown reason he didn't seem completely happy about this. Strange. Lloyd and I did much the same on the following Tuesday night to celebrate a 1-0 win at Blackburn. Again, I managed to lose my front door key. I didn't relish another telling off so instead of banging the front door at a similar time I slept in a tree in nearby gardens. I woke up with dew on me and a thumping headache. At about 8am I wandered back home, and my Mum opened the door and I just said "Oh, I stayed at Lloyds." After that I hid a key in the back garden for emergencies.

I missed our 1-0 defeat at Oldham as I was tempted by Lloyd to go to London for a night out. We went to some excellent pubs and then saw one near Soho with steps down into a bar. "Would you lads like to buy the singer a drink?" "Um, OK we said". The singer then sat down with us for two minutes then continued. Madonna she was not. We thought this was a terrible place and so went to leave but were presented with a massive bill – our pints were cheap but the "drink for the lady" was £20! We barely had that between us and there was a bouncer between us and the exit up the stairs. "Shove your money down your sock" said Lloyd and he used a bit of chat, which he was good at, to negotiate the bill down and we left with a torrent of abuse. Clearly all this all was great preparation for my o'level exams. I'd have been better off at Oldham I thought.

I wasn't going to miss our next one though, Middlesbrough at home as a win would surely guarantee our survival again. Amazingly the club had been involved in a promotion or relegation battle for 15 of the last 17 seasons. Des, his mate Mick, and I treated ourselves to the Arthur Wait seats and saw a poor first half which they shaded. The Croydon advertiser carried a photo of ever reliable Jim Cannon's winning header with Des and I already stood up ready to celebrate in the background.

Our final away trip was to Cardiff on the Inter-City via Reading. Young raw striker Galloway was outstanding as we condemned them to near certain relegation with a 3-0 victory, our biggest away win since 1978. "You lot must be rubbish mate, three down at home to us" Des shouted over at the home stand who were giving us stick for being "Dirty cockneys". We had a good pub crawl around Victoria to supplement the drinks on the Inter-City on the way home which happily seemed to disregard the "dry" label. I managed not to lose my door key, I felt very proud about that.

It was a shame we couldn't finish the season there. A dire 2-0 home defeat to Grimsby really didn't matter except for ensuring we had to play in the first round of the League cup next season. That weekend saw the horrific Bradford City fire disaster when 56 people were killed. Anyone who travelled the country supporting their team shuddered. That could have been us. There was another tragedy a couple of weeks later at the Heysel stadium during Liverpool's European Cup final against Juventus when 39 were killed. This led to all English clubs being banned from Europe. The event was shocking, but obviously wouldn't affect Palace we thought, we'll never get to a cup final, or finish high enough in the first division anyway.

We finished the season in 15th with 48 points which was no great improvement on previous seasons. With money still very tight it seemed unlikely anything would get better in the foreseeable future.

My season end statistics showed Aylott with nine being the top scorer, with Mahony on five. George Wood was the only ever present and Jim Cannon was my player of the season followed by Alan Irvine. The average home crowd was just

6,523. I also produced a graph showing our movement in league position over the season, the top half of the graph was not required.

Somehow despite going to all but 4 games this season, plus pool and drinking, I passed all my o'levels and that was school done. I guess that meant I would need to get a job, the purpose of which was of course to pay for the pub and more Palace trips but how I wished our fortunes would improve. The title of a Dire Straits track seemed appropriate for Palace though as good times still seemed "So far away".

But they wouldn't be as far away I as feared.

The dark days were soon to show some chinks of light, at long long last.

Chapter 5: 1985/86 – Moving out of the dark days.

1985 was a lively summer for me.

With not even Palace to keep me out the pub I upped my game on the drinking front. This generally meant the pool table Monday to Wednesday, a Thursday disco at the Fox pub with its curious smoky aroma and then trips to Brighton or London on Friday and Saturday nights. Sunday lunchtime was pool too as you got free crisps on the bar. Throw in Live Aid and the Ashes on TV, plus not too much exercise and it was no wonder I was getting a tiny bit chubby. The post pub grub stop was a regular stopping point but could make me sleepy, and I was regularly woken up by the same smiling policewoman on the steps of Three Bridges station around midnight. 1985 was not such a lively summer for Palace.

Manager Coppell was confident in a promising set of youngsters but felt a few additions were necessary despite the arrival of Steve Ketteridge from Wimbledon for £25,000, and the welcome resigning of Micky Droy. However, we did lose Jerry Murphy, the final link to our brilliant youth team of the late 1970's to Chelsea, and sadly Kevin Mabbutt to Coventry. I was not too confident at the start of the season with a squad looking weaker than last year and could only see yet another relegation battle ahead. We expected to sell just 1,500 season tickets.

There were two other developments. Firstly, our chairman Ron Noades was a leading figure behind a new football pools game "Top Score" where punters had to pick the top 6 scorers from 49 teams each week. This was supposed to earn clubs £50,000 a year. It's doubtful that it did. The second was the creation of a new cup competition for the top two divisions as clubs had no European football. Noades also had the unwelcome idea of banning away supporters "if you have no visitors you have no policing problems (or expenses)". That idea I didn't like at all.

In general football was in a bad place. The Bradford and Heysel disasters, hooliganism, European bans, and falling crowds in dilapidated stadiums gave it a very rough reputation. So much so that when I was filling in job applications the advice was not to mention that football was an interest of mine. There were some that even wanted the game banned!

I got my first job at Pallet Recovery in Crawley. I was to telephone companies, writing how many pallets each company needed collecting on index cards, not a stress-free role with my stammer. With no work experience at all my Mum dropped me off at a prefabricated office on my first day. I felt very nervous, and my first job was to make the tea. I was washing the mangers cup when it broke in my hand. As I looked at it I laughed, the mug was a Brighton one with a picture of their former striker Peter Ward grinning! There was no sign of Mullery in the picture.

Palace played Chelsea and West Ham in the highest profile friendlies, a late penalty saw us lose the first, but goals from Barber and Gray gave us a 2-1 win in the second.

Just before the season a few other players joined. Ken Hughes a backup goalkeeper, midfielder Andy Higginbottom, and Ian Wright a young striker from Greenwich Borough. Two of those would be pretty forgettable, one most certainly wouldn't be.

We started the season at Shrewsbury on a Sunday as a local flower show meant the police couldn't cope with both, but we did begin with a win! Goals in each half from Barber and Gray gave us a 2-1 victory. Droy and Cannon resumed their excellent defensive partnership and Ketteridge had a solid game on his debut. On the way back I found that a guy I chatted to in the ground, Alan, had money leant to him by Coppell as he was struggling for petrol to get home!

I didn't care that it was just one game, I produced my own league table, and we were 4th!

This season the Members scheme was introduced, with the idea of reducing crowd trouble. The Old Stand and the Sainsbury's terrace were renamed the Members Stand and Terrace with a £3 fee charged to join for which you got cheaper admission (£4.50 for a seat). Everyone still called them by their old names.

We made it a great start with a 1-0 win over Sunderland, who had Swindlehurst and ex Ipswich star Gates up front, with Droy powering in a header after 70 minutes. It seemed we had lost at Carlisle in our third game despite taking an early lead through Aylott but by the time Halpin put them 2-1 up with five minutes to go it looked grim. The confidence of the team shone through though and Barber got a last-minute equaliser to maintain our excellent start. Ian Wright was named as an unused sub for the first time but did get on in the next home game when we did lead Huddersfield 2-1, but eventually lost to a blistering late Webster strike and our optimism was dented.

Ian Wright started in the Milk Cup against Charlton after we had won the first leg 2-1. It looked dodgy when Palace old boy Flanagan put them ahead but thankfully the ever-dangerous Gray got us through with a 75th minute strike. Galloway replaced Wright from the bench and at this stage looked the better prospect. The second-round draw was interesting pairing us with Coppell's old friends at Manchester United for a two-legged second round tie.

I was left very disappointed on the following Saturday. We played Charlton again but had an off day and lost 3-1. They got two penalties to our one and we had dropped to 14th. After five years of struggle, I started to feel that we were never going to have much to cheer.

I decided not to go to as many games for a couple of months during which time I concentrated on playing pool with a friend Lloyd who had little football interest. I tried to find out if there was any drinking combination that meant I didn't wake up with a hangover. I never found one, although gin and tonic seemed the best bet.

This spell turned out to be one of the best periods for Palace since the turn of the decade. We signed full back Paul Brush initially on loan and then permanently from West Ham for £30,000, and Ken O'Doherty made the move Coppell had expected from the reserves to the first team. With Cannon and Droy as strong as ever and Wood dependable in goal we were starting to sound like a solid unit. We had some creditable home wins over Blackburn and Oldham and backed this up with a superb 3-1 win at Leeds with Tony Finnigan scoring a great individual goal, plus we managed away wins at Hull and Middlesbrough. The League cup tie against Manchester United saw them win both ties 1-0, Peter Barnes getting the winner at Selhurst. In both games Palace played well, and Coppell was said to be proud of his teams' efforts.

The biggest event at Palace during my self-imposed exile was a ground-share with Charlton who couldn't afford to stay at the Valley. Noades offered them the chance to share Selhurst Park, for a fee of course, otherwise Charlton may have folded so it seemed odd that Charlton took such a vehement dislike to us. It was an idea that caused much controversy, many Palace supporters not welcoming Charlton to our patch, and their fans forced away from their historical home to play at ours. We got some money, they survived, and ground sharing works for big clubs in Italy so why not here. I wasn't bothered.

After a couple of months I found some enthusiasm for football again and on a wet day when Palace weren't at home I went to Selhurst to watch Charlton v Carlisle. There was barely anyone there, but I realised how much I missed it. Also, my Dad was regularly saying how much we were improving so the following week I was back, for a Palace home game against Shrewsbury.

As soon as I stepped on to the Holmesdale terrace I bumped into Jay and also Paul Gifford, who I'd often chatted to at Norwood Junction. Feeling keen and refreshed I was glad to be back. "We are doing great" Jay said, "So much better, and ticker Taylor in midfield is very good". Paul was positive as well, so I leant on the crash barrier expecting another win. The game started under grey skies and never really got going, but I could see why Paul Brush had got good reviews and together with Cannon and Droy we did look organised at the back. Same old problem though, just couldn't score and when Hackett gave the Shrews the lead that was that. Nevertheless we were 6th, a position we maintained with a draw at Sunderland.

A morning boxing day kick-off meant I could get to Selhurst before our family do. It was cold and wet. A miserable lunchtime was complete when two goals from Cork gave Wimbledon a comfortable victory. I hoped for more joy on New Year's Day against Brighton but that was equally disappointing losing 2-0. The atmosphere was nasty walking back to the station, with even a gunshot being heard as we were climbing some steps close to Hove station. "Maybe it was a back-firing car" hoped Jay. Coppell and Noades both left before the end of the game to see Reading play Gillingham, hope was they would come back with a striker as whilst chances were created they were missed once again with Irvine, Barber and Finnigan the culprits.

My 1985 calendar year statistics showed the ever-reliable Jim Cannon leading the appearances list followed by Wood with two new boys on top of the goal scorers chart, Barber with 12 and Gray on 10. The average home crowd was only 6,954.

The dire weather meant the Saturday F.A. Cup third round tie against Luton was postponed to the Monday, a decision

Noades described as a "Bloody disgrace". I was none too chuffed having wasted a train fare as it was called off so late. The theory was that TV didn't want our game to damage the pitch further for the live match the next day when Charlton played West Ham. Our tie was played on the Monday night when nearly 10,000 saw us lose 2-1. Ian Wright and Andy Gray were both very lively but couldn't get past the experienced Steve Foster, who as an ex-Brighton captain got the inevitable stick from the crowd. With four injuries at full-back we signed Terry Howard on loan from Chelsea.

We broke a poor run when we played our ground-sharers Charlton with us as the home team. Wright got a start but struggled in a side that had lost a bit of confidence, but Finnigan and Taylor put us two up by half time. Reid did pull one back, but it was a valuable three points.

We decided to go by train to Huddersfield the following week, so I caught the 7.30 from Three Bridges on a perishing January morning. This was a struggle after a late night in the Moonraker the previous evening and I had a thumping headache on the train to London. I met Jay and Adi at Kings Cross and as our brag game started we noticed the outside world was getting whiter and icier. Adi had a small radio with a poor reception, and we kept hearing of various matches being called off. We changed trains at Sheffield and as it was blisteringly cold on the platform, we huddled into a shop to keep warm before being chucked out. As there was well over half an hour to wait we went to a pub, where we kept hearing more and more matches being called off. Eventually we realised that our game was one of very few north of Watford which was being played. On the train into Huddersfield there was ice appearing on the windows and the locals looked wrapped up for a hike across the arctic. When we got off there was a wind, the type of wind that seems to go through any number of layers you may have on. We were on a large open terrace with hills behind that this gale blew rapidly down and as Jay put it "This is an endurance test mate." We stood on it for half an hour even before kick-off and the 130 or so Palace fans began to stand closer together to at least minimise the effect of the cold. If someone brought a pie, which were of poor quality, or hot drink there was a scramble to try and stand as near to them as humanly possible for the few extra degrees. Perhaps the game will warm us up? Think again, it was 0-0 with Cannon and Droy superb at the back. I've never been happier to be back on a train. We sprinted to seats closest to a heater and got the cards out and were pleased it was only a brief change at Wakefield Westgate on the way back. Then some good news, it was not an alcohol-free train and the buffet was open. We tucked right in.

Getting back to away games plus spending most nights out meant I needed to supplement my income still further. I therefore decided to take a slight risk and operate a bit of a betting service. I gave odds for matches in division one and two plus various bets on the Palace game of the day. I made sure I paid out if someone won but had forgotten which frequently happened, all good for the reputation. It worked well and I made a small profit. Enough to fund a couple of away games each season.

Ian Wright had forced his way into the team and was looking very raw, but Coppell clearly had faith in him, as he had displaced Aylott who had asked to go on to the transfer list and ended up at Barnsley on loan.

Norwich arrived at Selhurst Park and lived up to their top of the table status and played us off the park to lead 2-0 at half time. It didn't help that Droy was injured, replaced by Nebbeling who had improved after a loan spell at Northampton. Barber pulled one back leaving Coppell to complain that "we stood off them too much, they aren't Juventus!"

The following Saturday saw the nadir as far as league crowds go, for a standard 3pm kick off we attracted only a bedraggled

3,775 for the game against Carlisle who were relegation certainties. It was a miserable, bitterly cold day with rain throughout including a dramatic deluge in the second half. The first half was dire and only the goal from Gray prevented the half time boos. The swap of Wright for Higginbottom didn't make much difference, indeed Carlisle equalised and could easily have nicked all three points. A desperate afternoon and one-star performance of which Coppell said, "If we don't work hard we won't even beat Carlisle". After the game Palace had a bizarre midweek trip to the Middle East to play the Qatar Under 21 team, the game ended 0-0 in front of just 200.

The pitch wasn't helping. It was becoming a quagmire after a very cold and wet patch with two teams now playing on it. There was talk of installing a Luton style artificial surface, but Coppell said, "I hate them". That was pretty much end of discussion. A further option was under pitch heating, but the £70,000 price tag didn't make it attractive to thrifty Uncle Ron. We then lost another match to the weather against Portsmouth.

Next up was a trip to Blackburn with Jay, Adi, and I on a three-and-a-half-hour rail jaunt via Preston. The police escorted walk from the station to the ground on yet another cold day took us past a garage with a local working on a car. In perky mood after a good win at cards on the way up I piped up with "Look boys, that's a rare sight." Eyes turned towards me "A northerner at work." The mechanic wasn't impressed, the rest of the Palace crowd, and the policeman near me, giggled. In very poor conditions it wasn't a great game, but I took advantage of the pies that got a glowing recommendation from Jay "…better than the crap at Huddersfield." Andy Gray put us ahead and with conditions worsening it looked likely we would hold on, but Glenn Keeley equalised. Then Ian Wright, on as a sub for Finnigan (before he got sent off after some dubious challenges) grabbed a late winner to enable us to warm up with mass sprints around the vast open spaces on the big away terrace. You'd have thought we'd won the cup not won in front of 4,772 at Blackburn. There was a distinct improvement in the team from a year ago, we would have lost a game like this then. The younger brigade of Gray, Barber and Wright were offering so much more than our strikers over the last four years. The train was serving alcohol from Preston, so I tucked into the cans of gin and tonic. There was a bit of a "down in one" competition going on with some lads with beers and one said to me I bet you couldn't do that with a spirit. I bet I could I thought. I asked what the bet was "I'll buy you another if you do, you buy me one if you don't." I downed it, a walk in the park and got my drink. In strength terms it was nothing compared to our family do's. I did this a couple more times and would have carried on had we not arrived back in London. "Oooh Pubs open," said Adi.

George Wood missed his first league game since he joined nearly three years ago against Middlesbrough, his was replacement Steve Hardwick on loan from Oxford. We went behind to a Bernie Slaven goal, he had contacted all English clubs the previous year to find a club. Shame we didn't step in as Middlesbrough had as he looked lively throughout. Kevin Taylor, impressing again in midfield, equalised with an excellent strike from a free kick. Then with the game drifting towards a draw on came Ian Wright, full of pace and energy and a "why wasn't I on earlier" attitude and it took him just five minutes to slam home Gray's astute header for three points. Gray had a face full of relief having missed an earlier penalty.

There were rumours around that Palace were considering a merger with Wimbledon. They arose from public meetings being held by both clubs but Noades clarified the position "You have my word there is no link between Wimbledon and Palace." Indications were the Palace meeting was about a new form of finance.

The usual crew made their way up to Oldham the following week on a smart Inter-City train via Manchester Piccadilly for £12.50. We were now regularly joined by Paul Gifford, who unlike Jay, Adi, and I, was in his last year at school so was on a tight budget. Paul's outlay was strictly train fare, match entrance (£2.50 at Oldham), a strict number of cigarettes and the cheapest possible lunch and hopefully not a big loss at brag. When a transfer bus, included in the fare much to Paul's relief, picked us up from Oldham station it was only about midday. It was cool and windy, and we didn't relish the prospect of the bus going straight to the ground. We needn't have worried, the Police came on board and said we were going to be dropped off at a pub for a couple of hours. Cue chants of "We love the police, we do". Not only was it a pub, but a cracking one and we were soon playing pool with friendly locals with a varied juke box, although Paul took a dim view of the Madonna tunes. I got a bit too excited and ordered two pints straight away for me and drinks for the others and I carried on downing them at a rapid pace before the bus came back to drop us off at Boundary Park. I was staggering and was worried I wouldn't get in. Luckily the Police smiled at me, "Having a good day son?" and turned a blind eye. The game was forgettable, particularly to me in my state, and we lost to a goal in each half. We gave up towards the end and had a competitive game of throwing stones from the decaying terrace into a plastic cup. I didn't enjoy the trip back, for reasons I tried to deny I felt awful, terrible headache and tired. I was desperate for food, but the buffet car had run out and the squeaking trolley was nowhere to be seen. I resorted to a McDonalds at Victoria not fancying at all the drinks Jay and Paul were enjoying and thought that'll be the last time I tuck into drinking before the game, and it was.

Any very distant hopes of promotion went the following week with a 1-0 defeat to Stoke, with the crowd suddenly dropping to just 4,576. We had most of the play but Stoke defended well with Steve Bould, plus George Berry and his hair, very solid after Bertschin's first half headed goal.

My cousin Graham joined us for the ever-popular trip to Fulham, who were in the relegation zone now they had lost the likes of Lewington, Houghton, Davies, and Brown. Ninety minutes later they were bottom as we ran out 3-2 winners with Wright, a handful throughout, getting the winner thanks to a defensive blunder which was duly celebrated by a large Palace following largely in ski hats. "Seven points behind third" Graham said. Promotion? Well, you never know!

Wright was now firmly established in the team, so Steve Galloway was allowed to leave for Cambridge on loan. I thought he was a handy squad player particularly with his pace supplementing what we already had. Meanwhile full back Gary Lock left too, for Sweden having lost his place in the team.

Next up was the big rivalry. In these days a little edge had gone out of the Brighton games and the crowd was just 9,184. We got our first win over them since October 1978 (When we scored two quick goals, the second of those from Swindlehurst, bringing one of the loudest celebrations I've heard). This time an early goal from Paul Brush settled a low-key game with a fine free kick. Kevin Taylor had a good game doing a fine job of marking Brighton's midfielder Danny Wilson who Coppell had rated "the best in the division." Gavin Nebbeling had come in for an injured Droy and with Cannon's stabling influence they have formed a solid partnership. There had been a move to bring in Larry May from Barnsley, but no need now.

This win gave me the opportunity to poke fun at the Brighton supporting Manager of Pallet Recovery Services, Bob Still, despite his kind efforts to pick me up each morning. It was proving a fun job! In the summer Bob brought a TV into the office. He said "Right, let's get the work done by 11, Simon hit the phones, and Tony sort the drivers out." I was a little baffled "What's the rush today?" I asked assistant Manager Tony. "You'll see" he said. I found out that at 11am office work finished, and the Test Match went on TV and we sat there with tea and biscuits. At lunch Bob even went out to get fish and chips, plus donuts for the tea break. If one of the big bosses appeared from head office Bob had arranged for the repairers to give us a knock on the door. At that point, the TV, went off, phones were picked up and fake calls made. As the boss walked in Bob would say in a surprised tone "Oh, 'ello Mr 'arris, good to see you". As soon as he left it was back to Richie Benaud and Jim Laker.

Another derby followed and a big Palace crowd made their way to the ramshackled Plough Lane at Wimbledon. We lost 5-0 at home to them last season but our far more vibrant team fought back from a Fashanu (our former loanee) opener to level through Wright. Coppell was pleased "We did have a mental block against them, but this was a smashing game with a good atmosphere." This draw was well received by our ground-sharers Charlton who remained in the promotion places just ahead of Wimbledon. They should specifically thank Jim Cannon for a great last-minute goal line clearance, meaning that we were in the mix too. We were just three points from the top three so Graham's post Fulham optimism was well founded. That was emphasised by a 2-1 over a physical Bradford team although Coppell was quick to pour come realism on our dreams "We have no chance of going up."

These hopes of getting into the top three promotion places were boosted by the traditional victory over Portsmouth, with Andy Gray scoring all three goals in a 2-1 win. We now have 13 points from 15! This season is a massive improvement on the last five with Gray, proving a bargain at £2,000, starting to form an exciting forward partnership with Wright. A stark contrast to some of the lumbering forwards of the recent past.

The Public meeting Palace had advertised took place on 3 April at Fairfield Halls and there was a high degree of mystery about an event advertised as "one of the most important meetings in the Eagles history." I went along with Jay and Paul and heard the idea was to set up a Lifeline scheme, the premise was for supporters to pay £2 a week for a heap of benefits such as discounts in various stores, the club shop, match ticket discounts, availability of executive facilities, holiday vouchers and an annual cash prize of up to £50,000. All profits from this would go into strengthening the team with £140,000 available if 2,500 people joined. The club would also form a new company "Crystal Palace (1986) Ltd" with Noades explaining "We have formed a new company that will play in the league next season. Any financial backing that we can raise for the company would not be taken by our bankers to reduce our loan liabilities, instead it would be available for Steve to try and get us promoted." The scheme, which had been used at Bolton, was well received and seemed to offer good value to supporters and the wider public, whilst giving us an edge in the transfer market.

Our hopes of the top three were dealt a hammer blow at Grimsby. A Cannon own goal was followed by Taylor being sent off for an elbow on Peake, who promptly got a second goal to finish us off. A dodgy late penalty made it 3-0. We had treated ourselves to seats in the splendid Findus Stand which gave a cracking view of the gloomy events. "Once we are in the first division, we may not come here again," said Jay. We had paid the £9.50 for the club train, which carried about 300. Paul's day was made by a nearby cheap superstore for lunch. I told Paul "Oy, Pikey, you've got enough for a round at Victoria now". Paul went pale at the thought.

Our very distant promotion hopes remained with a 3-0 thrashing of Leeds, who looked tired and one of the worst teams seen at Selhurst this season. The pace of Wright, who got the first, troubled them constantly with the excellent Alan Irvine getting the other two to break his 28-game run of non-scoring.

The trip to Millwall was less traumatic than we endured for the FA Cup match last season, but Jay, Paul and I still felt very edgy before getting into the small covered terrace largely due to some heavy shoving and shouting on the platform at East Croydon station. The single young Policeman didn't look keen to get involved in that and instead crept up the slope leading up to the ticket barriers. The match was one sided, Nebbeling gifting them the first with a poor back pass having nearly done the same minutes earlier thanks to a sodden pitch. Sheringham scored a cracking drive, and our old friend Lovell made it 3-0. Millwall though stopped playing, and late goals from Higginbottom and then Ketteridge gave us a chance of an unlikely point and Wright so nearly got it from Finnigan's free kick. "Oh well, safer walk back now," said Jay.

We were joined by Kenton for the trip to Barnsley to see Palace at their best. We went behind early on but led by half-time thanks to Ian Wright whose pace ripped their defence to shreds. We were stood on the top corner of the open terrace quite near the seated home fans, who were not happy and seemed to take a great dislike to Wright. They were bursting with hate when he scored the second, with various gestures and screaming, and then turned their scorn on to us. Once they quietened Jay casually shouted over "Mate, turn round – you'll miss his hat-trick goal in a minute." That didn't calm them down. They did equalise after half time but Aylott, on loan at Oakwell just weeks previously, came on and got a third before Ketteridge polished off a 4-2 win.

A meeting was held in the week in which agreement was reached to introduce a play-off system next season. This meant that those finishing 3rd, 4th, and 5th in the second division would compete with the from 4th bottom first division team in two legged semi-finals and final to decide who goes up or stays up. It was not lost on us that if that had been in place this season, we would likely have faced Leicester in a play-off semi-final. Some were frustrated, but it showed the progress we had made from our four previous seasons.

The final game was meaningless, we would finish 5th whatever. Andy Higginbottom put us ahead against Sheffield

United who equalised towards the end in a typical end of season game. The highlight of which was some lighthearted banter with former Palace keeper John Burridge by us folks in the Sainsbury's end (oops, Member's terrace).

My player of the year was Jim Cannon. Irvine and Cannon made most appearances with Barber and Gray with 11 heading the scoring charts. The average home league crowd of 6,904 was still disappointing, our highest was only 11,731 against Portsmouth.

This had been a very good season. There was more pace and vitality in the team with Wright and Gray, and with Wood, Cannon, Droy and Brush providing the experience at the back we looked a well-structured team. Over a pint after the game there was considerable optimism for next season. "I can't wait another minute" by Five Star played in the pub. It summed up how I felt.

Chapter 6: 1986/87 – Legends combine

For the first time in many years there was optimism before the start of a season.

It wasn't that we added a procession of expensive players, but the form of last season indicated better times ahead. Only Anton Otulakowski joined, for £19,000 from Millwall with Coppell declaring "not to waste the lifeline money". There were pundits predicting us to be in the thick of the promotion battle, I thought we could again manage top six but wasn't sure if we had enough in the squad to make promotion. Gray and Wright were pacy but there was a lack of height up front, also the midfield needed more options although Taylor and Ketteridge were decent.

We lost Henry Hughton on a free transfer, he had been a valuable player over the years, and I was disappointed that he had gone to Brentford initially on loan. Trevor Aylott also departed for Bournemouth also on loan.

It's often who you keep that is as important as who you acquire and hearing that Jim Cannon had signed a new two-year deal was very good news. Big Jim felt there was a good chance this season "We finished 5th last year and if we do so again we'll be in the play-offs. I don't think the standard of the league is that high and if we can add some experience we will be in with a shout." His partner at the back, veteran Micky Droy, had also said he could manage one more year.

Despite playing against Chelsea's dynamic front pair of Dixon and Speedie we won our highest profile friendly 2-1 plus put four past Fulham. Jay and I had a trip to the Southend friendly, which we lost but had beers in the sun.

That summer I left Pallet Recovery for a job with brighter prospects, so I spent a Saturday with friend Lloyd going round stacks of employment agencies to register. With the clock getting close to 5pm Lloyd was bored and persuaded me to walk past the last agency, Reed. I then made probably the best decision of my life. I said to him "Look I'll meet you in the Moonraker later, I'm going to register at Reed." Two days later Reed offered me an interview at an "International Shipping Conference called TACA". After a nervous first interview I was eventually taken to see the acting chairman, David. He looked very daunting sitting in his office and asked me some standard interview questions. Then he said "Oh, you like football!" and we chatted about the Mexico World Cup for ages. He looked at me and said, "What money do you want?" I said £5,500, he agreed easily. Dam, I should have said £7,000 I thought! The office looked highly professional, and I felt a bit apprehensive that I would be working there.

Since the Palace fixtures came out, I had been looking forward to our opening match at Barnsley. Then disaster. A distant relative was getting married. Surely I didn't need to go? I didn't know them! But apparently for inexplicable reasons my attendance was deemed essential. I was not impressed. The wedding couple got divorced very soon after. I was even less impressed.

During my first week at TACA I was told to sit opposite Andy Willmott. He started our first chat asking which team I supported "Crystal Palace" I said. He tried not to laugh. "You?" I asked "Guess!" I thought please don't be Brighton. I went through a few then got to "West Ham?" He nodded. They had finished third in the first division last season and with Cottee and McAvennie up front were a very good team. He was to become a lifelong best friend.

That afternoon I had a driving test, my fourth. I passed it and as I walked into the office Andy said, "Fancy going to Manchester United on Monday?" I said our next game was Stoke at home so looked mystified. "No, West Ham are playing there" OK I said. Then he convinced me the best way to become a better driver was to drive to Manchester which I naively agreed to. The match was amazing, with some great football from both teams who seemed to be playing a different game to Palace, with Andy's boys winning 3-2. On the way home the weather turned from sunshine to a deluge. As we made our way down the M1 I was struggling to see out of the window with a storm lashing the windscreen. Andy was asleep and I didn't want to wake him. Eventually I found out that contrary to what I thought the M1 did not end at the M25 and it instead took you into Central London. Andy woke up "Where the hell are we?" We got back after a six-hour trip.

On Saint and Greavsie, the Saturday lunchtime ITV show which made great post pub viewing, they had us as second division favourites and Ian Wright predicted as the second division top scorer. Wow, we were making progress! We were already fourth having beaten Stoke.

That evening I went to Andy's hometown Crowborough to have a few beers. The house was big and had a steep drive. His Mum answered the door and off we went. We did drink a lot that night in the Blue Anchor, The Cross, White Hart, and the Rose of Bengal curry house. Andy had forgotten a key but said his Dad would have stayed up to let us in. His Dad turned out to be David, the daunting interviewer. I felt a bit awkward but five minutes later David was serving me much needed ham sandwiches, crisps, and cups of tea. Andy was asleep on the floor.

Palace's third game was at Bradford and would be played at the rugby ground as Valley Parade had been decimated by the terrible fire last year. There was no train so Jay, Paul and I went on the coach which took five hours. The away end was uncovered seating with a big fence at the front and we were some distance from the pitch. With just 3,856 turning up we went behind in the first minute in a game played with a 2020 lockdown atmosphere. A lucky deflection from Irvine's shot produced an equaliser. Ketteridge got the winner six minutes from the end resulting in a massive celebration and in the chaos, I got a cut on my arm on the big fence. The journey home could have been better, Spike the PA man and travel supervisor was sick on the coach. Not an ideal aroma with four hours left.

We were second, with nine points out of nine. We are coming to get you I told Andy but then shuddered at how good they looked at Old Trafford. I went to see West Ham, using David's season ticket, for their next home game against Nottingham Forest. Andy celebrated with his elbows everywhere when McAvennie scored, and the noise seemed deafening after years of dwindling Selhurst crowds. Forest ended up winning 2-1.

I drove to my first Palace away game at Derby with Jay, Adi, Paul, and Kenton all of whom took various forms of alcohol with them. I always enjoyed the baseball ground, very atmospheric but we lost to a late John Gregory penalty, and also Irvine to a hamstring strain.

I suggested Andy came to our next home game, Huddersfield at home and he joined the rest of us on the Sainsburys terrace. He looked shocked at how few people were in the ground, although for us it was a decent 6,638 gate for an evening game. I'm not too sure if he felt West Ham would be under undue threat if we did go up either, although we won with a goal bundled in by Droy at the Holmesdale end. We were lucky that George Wood was on fine form in goal and had been taking advantage of the tips Coppell had picked up on keeper training at the recent World Cup.

Moves for greater security at Selhurst had increased, whether this was linked to the upcoming home game with Millwall was not clarified but CCTV and extra fencing was being installed.

There was considerable optimism before the arrival of Sheffield United on a chilly and damp afternoon. We put in a below par performance though and got beat 2-1 missing Otulakowski. Coppell's hopes of a good performance getting crowds closer to five figures were dashed "There was only one team in it, and they looked like they were the only ones who wanted to win in the first half". We got worse at Portsmouth, in the new Full Members Cup, getting hammered 4-0 in front of a mere 2,685.

Next up was a £12 train trip to Blackburn, and what a disastrous trip it was. The train took over four and a half hours and was so late we didn't get into Ewood Park until halfway through the first half. After the game there was crowd trouble with groups of Blackburn fans charging up the side streets taking punches at our supporters' group despite us having a police escort. The journey back was even longer, and it was a dry train so the pub at Victoria was much in need. Palace at least put on a good show, we missed Taylor's goal but Gray secured the points at the end to leave us second in the league, but then put in a transfer request as he was disappointed not to be getting a regular start.

We could have gone top of the league with a win, but we lost again at Selhurst on the following Saturday against Reading 3-1 in a physical game. Gray was sent off just after their defender Baillie suffered the same fate for a head butt on Ian Wright. We were unlucky hitting the woodwork four times and Coppell was dissatisfied with referee Bodenham's performance "He sent Gray off for punching a player in the face, which he denies. For some of the bookings I think some should be put up for a mystery prize". The ref was from Brighton.

Millwall were our next visitors, and that didn't start well with Sheringham giving them an early lead. Typically, against the Lions there were crowd issues, and the game was held up for five minutes before half time as for some reason about 200 of them ran on to the pitch. I wrote to the club to complain that many Millwall fans were allowed just to wander into the Arthur Wait home enclosure. The afternoon improved considerably in the second half, Otulakowski back after injury levelled and

Finnigan got the winner to put us top – yes, top of the league! Wow, what an improvement over the last 18 months.

The following day Noades said "Fencing, over five feet high, will be installed to help to control crowds." After Saturday most agreed it was a good idea and could not see what harm high fencing could possibly cause. Meanwhile the club agreed a £100,000 three-year sponsorship deal with AVR All Star Video's, and young Richard Shaw signed a professional contract.

The following week I went to Bury for the second leg of our second round League (Littlewoods) cup tie, enjoying a near five hour journey each way. Noades was on the away terrace too and was very chatty with supporters. It was a poor performance, but we got through and avoided extra time with Wright's winner from Stebbing's through ball.

Four days later Jay and Paul came with me for a drive to Leeds. With heavy traffic we took over five hours to get there, including a stop which left Paul unimpressed with the cost of the bacon rolls. We stood on the terrace parallel to the penalty area and watched Palace get hammered 3-0. We had been riding our luck at times this season and with Sheridan pulling the strings in midfield we were rarely in the match. We decided to edge towards the exit as injury time approached to beat the traffic. It didn't work. We had parked in a big rough car park next to the ground, and it took nearly two hours to escape. Jay and Paul even had time to get some tinnies, then more tinnies, which meant numerous toilet stops on the way home.

During the week the Police announced they wanted the Arthur Wait enclosure closed "If the area is a problem it should be eliminated" said Chief Super Intendent Gregory. Palace secretary Alan Leather responded by explaining the problems against Millwall were caused by their supporters deliberately seeking access into the home areas. On the playing scene

Palace were looking at two strikers, Mark Bright from Leicester who has first division experience and Walsall's David Kelly about whom Coppell said, "was out of our price range." What a stroke of luck that turned out to be.

I went to Wembley for the first time to see England beat Northern Ireland 3-0 with Andy. He introduced me to a couple of fantastic pubs in Baker Street, The Globe and The Allsop Arms. I enjoyed the night out but cast an eye around thinking how amazing it would be to see Palace here in a cup final. "Your dreaming" Andy said, I reluctantly agreed as we stopped off for a couple more pints in Victoria meaning we turned up very late at work. Luckily people didn't worry about that sort of thing at TACA. Indeed, timings there were let's say flexible. Let's take lunch. In my first week Andy, I, and two colleagues Joanne and Don went to the Sun pub just over the road about 12.30. We had a couple of pints and with an hour gone I said, "Shall we head back then". "No!" said Don "I have to buy a drink first". We had that. Then Joanne brought one. I was feeling wobbly when one of the big bosses came over. How am I going to explain getting sacked for being drunk in my first week when I get home I thought as we had been out for way over two hours by now. As the boss reached us I said "Hello Mike, sorry I think we have been out a little longer than an hour…" He just said, "I don't care, you folks want a drink?" Andy said yes and we had that, brought one for Mike then got back to the office well after 4pm. This was not a rare occurrence. When I got home trolleyed my Mum just said, "I don't know how you get these jobs". It was pretty dam good.

There was little improvement from the Leeds game when we travelled on the £7 train to Birmingham. It was very clear we needed a big striker to hold the ball up and now we had lifeline money available there was growing impatience that we hadn't signed one. We lost 4-1, not the best day for Jim Cannon to celebrate his 500th game commemorated by a trophy presented by DJ Spike. The food in the ground was the highlight of the day but we slipped to 5th with Coppell not happy with the depth of the squad. I wasn't happy having to endure "Every loser wins" by Nick Berry twice as we waited to escape St Andrews.

We only attracted 4,856 for the Shrewsbury game and our usual group was joined by James Hirchfield, who became universally known as "Clubby" as he had all possible merchandise. We watched a dire performance that was more reminiscent of our struggles of a couple of years ago and the score line could have been worse than the 3-2 defeat. I was pissed off after this. I thought we had been making progress, but we were rubbish today. As I walked down the Holmesdale Road after the game, I kicked a coke hard can down the near deserted road in frustration listening to it scrape against the tarmac. Sadly, the can wasn't empty so I got wet jeans too. Not a good day.

There was a further member of our group when Danny Whitmarsh appeared for the third-round League cup tie against first division Nottingham Forest. Having seen them beat West Ham earlier in the season and bearing in mind the poor form we were in I feared a thrashing. However, we improved and took the lead twice through Irvine and Gray, but a penalty from Pearce and a miskick from Birtles got them a draw. "How did you do against Forest?" I asked Andy with relish. A very good effort, as Forest were top of the first division. I thought Jonny Method was formidable in midfield. We would face a replay at Forest. I should copy and paste that sentence for future use.

Plymouth away had weekend trip written all over it, so Jay and I went down on the Friday for a steak and drinks on the Hoe and stayed at the very decent Warren Park Hotel. We woke a little hungover with confusion over how many pubs we had got to. We met James and Paul at the game where we stood on a big open terrace and saw us get beat 3-1 which left us in mid-table which was so disappointing after such a bright start. Coppell was not impressed with our defending "What do you expect, we have the worst back line in the division" He barked rather unfairly. Jay and I had booked another night out, at the decent Kildare B&B and we consoled ourselves with a splendid curry and a lighter drinking session whilst the others were suffering a freezing two-hour delay on the way back to London.

Jay Thayre joined us for the replay at Forest, we played well and just a late Nigel Clough goal gave them the win. Coppell played Nebbeling in place of Droy for this one, and shortly afterwards Micky left for a loan spell at Brentford. He had been a great asset for a couple of years, but age was catching up with him.

More depression came along thanks to our fifth league defeat in a row, this time a 3-0 thrashing by Grimsby. We were very poor and many of the 5,000 sung "what a load of rubbish" and departed well before the end. Looking round Selhurst with massive swathes of empty terrace space and deserted seats the ground looked sad. The last few minutes made us feel that all hope of promotion this, or any year, had just been a pipedream. The miserable walk in the darkness, and heavy rain, back to Norwood Junction summed up the mood. Jay, Adi, and I were saying we were giving up and not going for months if this is all they can serve up. Ten minutes later we turned round, walked back up the road, and booked to go to Oldham.

At last we made a signing, and it was to be a very significant one. Mark Bright joined for £75,000 from Leicester with the arrangement being an initial loan. Coppell was hopeful "Obviously we are in a bit of a hole at the moment, but I hope Mark can be the catalyst and spark a reaction from the team as a whole."

After the Grimsby fiasco we faced Ipswich, and few were optimistic, but it turned out to be one of our best performances of the season. It started badly with Kevin Wilson putting the farmers two up but in an exciting game Wright got a last-ditch equaliser and it finished 3-3. Bright scored on his debut and although it was only a draw it was a hugely improved performance and the celebration for the equaliser was manic making it a much happier walk into Croydon for a pint.

Our trip to Oldham happily included a trip to the excellent pub, which I enjoyed a little too much last season. The landlord said he "expected and welcomed the friendly Palace fans" and we again had a better time there than at the game. We lost 1-0 despite dominating it after conceding an early goal. We got a £2 reduction on the rail fare in view of the Plymouth delay, Jay and I didn't mention that we spent that evening happily eating and drinking on the Hoe. Back in Victoria we found Pizza Hut were offering a new "Eat all you want" buffet. We most certainly did. A much-needed diet could wait.

Palace did improve after that, beating Sunderland 2-0 with a goal after just 18 seconds from Finnigan, and the excellent Bright adding a second. Not that it lasted, as Jay and I saw us drop to 15th with a defeat at Portsmouth. The highlight of the trip was the excellent Barnham Hotel Pub where a good few beers and winner-stays-on pool table were enjoyed, until Jay pointed out some locals were not happy that we kept winning so we beat a hasty retreat to lose some money at Hove dog track.

We finally clicked against Hull, a fantastic 5-1 victory to raise spirits at long last. With Finnigan superb and Nebbeling showing why Coppell had the confidence to allow Droy to leave. To make the day even better the former captain of our bitterest rivals Brighton, and Hull's manager, Brian Horton, was sent off. It was a happy day and as we left the ground XTC's "Senses working overtime" had appropriate lyrics.

The Huddersfield trip last year was a freezefest, so we hoped for better when we made the trip from Kings Cross via Wakefield Westgate. It seemed very cold and bleak yet again when (not Alan) Shearer put them ahead after a deflection off big Jim which came just after Kevin Taylor was sent off by George Courtney for retaliation. With Bright, now looking a £75,000 bargain and linking play superbly, we still looked in with a chance and when they made a hash of a clearance he was on hand to equalise, and then head in a winner from Irvine's free kick. He is just the target man we have been so desperate for.

The Brighton rivalry popped up on Boxing day and fussy referee David Elleray made it a stop start affair. Happily, we beat them again with Irvine scoring from Barber's cross just after half time. Wright came on and joined Bright up front and the seaweed struggled to cope, leaving Barber to settle the game. We held on comfortably as Jasper had been sent off during the second half.

The next day we collapsed at impressive Ipswich, losing 3-0 in front of a big Palace contingent but made up for it on New Year's Day 1987 at WBA with Barber getting the first, and a perfect chip by Bright winning it with five minutes to go. I was struggling desperately with a hangover and drank endless cups of black tea so much so the mumsy server gave me a couple of freebies and a brownie.

I produced some 1986 statistics with Cannon on top of the appearances list and Wright top of the goalscoring chart. I was proud that I had been to every away game.

We still needed to improve the team and there was talk of the successful lifeline scheme being extended to give Coppell £200,000 to spend. He did fork out in the week in a deal to sign defender Gary O'Reilly for £40,000 from Brighton. Coppell's idea was a straight exchange for Aylott, but they weren't keen.

We won again this time against Derby, thanks to Gray's goal and outstanding performance, with a healthy 9,560 showing up. Cannon played heroically, battling through with a badly swollen face for most the game. Jay's favourite Stebbing was having a decent run in the team, luckily for me he regularly bet with me on him to score first. He rarely looked like troubling my bank balance.

Our form must have concerned Brian Clough, who despite a fabulous career had never won the F.A. Cup as Football Focus went on and on about before our third-round clash. Well, he still won't. We beat Forest, who were 4th in the first division, on a snowy slippery pitch with a fine goal from Irvine who had arrived late because of icy roads.

The weather that week was awful, with massive amounts of snow around Crawley. I lived locally to the TACA office and took over an hour to walk in wearing my Canadian boots. There was very little work to do so Andy and I had pie and chips and many lunchtime beers agreeing on a bet on who of Palace or West Ham would finish higher in their respective divisions. I was desperate to get promoted and play them.

I was writing letters regularly to the Croydon Advertiser around now, one declared 1987 will be year to remember and a second how well the lifeline money was being spent. Well, we'll see I guess.

My letters looked a load of rubbish when we lost 1-0 at home to Barnsley. We looked sluggish and were back to the days of dreadful finishing. MacDonald got a late deflating winner for them and we went into Crystals for beers.

We travelled to Tottenham in the fourth round of the Cup. A proper big game and a proper test. They had our old foe Clive Allen up front too. The away end was packed. Seriously packed. So much so that Jay's feet weren't even touching the terrace. We thought it was a good laugh, and after all the banks of space at Selhurst it did make a change. A guy behind me did start to become a bit concerned for his young son but it was all still good humoured, despite the big fences in front of us. There was a cracking atmosphere but Palace were outclassed, and whilst some goals were unlucky a 4-0 defeat was fair enough. Allen got a penalty too. I was depressed after the game as it emphasised the massive gap between us and the first division. With an improved but still modest transfer kitty I found it hard to see how we could get anywhere close to the level of Tottenham. We had that chance in 1979 but it seems we have blown it, particularly if we can't increase our crowds of still only around 6,500.

We lost our way a little after that with a convincing defeat at Stoke. I drove their feeling very proud of my new graphic equaliser which Jay and Paul (to a lesser degree as he wasn't great fan of UB40, Pepsi & Shirley and the Pretenders) enjoyed with copious beers and scotch in the car.

We also decided to set up a five a side football team just for the summer when we barely saw each other, clearly tactics needed to be discussed in the pub over the next few weeks. That one summer turned into eighteen years. My first signing was to be Andy, who I knew would be our best player and I convinced him to join us from another team. Life at TACA was great fun, the place felt more like a social club. On our colleague Don's birthday the office came to a standstill as Andy had arranged a striper, dressed as a nurse, to come into the office during the afternoon to help him celebrate. He needed no encouragement.

We then only drew at home to struggling Bradford who should have won, before Reading away which was an interesting one. The obligatory Trevor Senior goal put us behind, but with three minutes to go Ketteridge was fouled in the box and referee Lloyd pointed to the spot. Then Reading convinced Lloyd to speak to the linesman and a dubious offside was given and the penalty cancelled. A large Palace crowd were not happy. Danny looked set to explode, "not the time to tell him it's just a game?" Jay whispered to me.

The following week Palace hit the headlines as a merger with first division Wimbledon (and possibly Charlton) was mooted. This was clearly a very sensitive issue. Wimbledon chairman

Sam Hamman was determined to move from Plough Lane, and we saw another route to the first division. Noades said he would only sanction such a merger, on which detailed talks had been held, if:

The name of the team contains Crystal Palace.

The management is from Crystal Palace.

We play in the first division.

The plan must have the approval of the majority of Palace fans.

It became difficult to establish what, other than the ground move, Wimbledon would gain from this.

Jim Cannon was against it feeling it would lead to unfair dismissal claims as many players would be kicked out as one club couldn't support the playing staff of two.

Feelings on this were running high as we beat Blackburn. There was a 30-minute demonstration after the game which included chants of "Noades Out" and "We don't want a merger". Jay and I thought the criticism of Noades was unjustified, he was remaining impartial and had given the supporters the choice. The questionnaire handed out before the game asked various key questions including:

If independent, when do you think we could win promotion?

I said 3 seasons.

Would you support the team if it takes longer?

I said Yes.

Are you in favour of a merger?

I said Yes.

If you are in favour, are you convinced?

I said No.

Having studied responses which showed 80% of people to be against the merger Noades called Hamman on 6 March and called it off and made it clear that Palace was not for sale. Noades was also getting stick for not putting a roof on the Holmesdale Terrace but he explained that it was considered in 1982 when it would have cost £470,000 so the idea was rejected.

The following Friday night Jay and I had a lengthy snooker session at Paul's in Oxted. After a few beers we struggled out the door for a cold 6.50am start for our trip to Shrewsbury. We got the 8.35 to Wolverhampton with Jay saying something awful about the hair of a dog. I had coffee. We changed trains and got to Shrewsbury very early. Then a sympathetic policeman told us our game was off, which wasn't a great surprise as it was blizzarding. We then considered which match to go to instead, I fancied Liverpool v Luton, we all rejected the local but dull sounding games at Birmingham and WBA, and so settled on Coventry v Sheffield Wednesday to "get the ground". In those days it was great as you could just pick a game, even at Liverpool, as they were very rarely sold out in advance. We caught a train from Shrewsbury back to Wolverhampton, then Wolverhampton to Birmingham then Birmingham to Coventry. By then it was 2.55 so we got a taxi and joined the Wednesday fans in the away end. I was very cold, so I got a pie to warm me up. I bit into it and the base fell out and I had gravy and lumps of meat of dubious quality all over my new white trainers. Jay laughed. I brought another pie in a bad temper. The dull game in awful conditions, was won 1-0 by Coventry. We were all cheered up by the joyful news that Brighton were now bottom of our league. Amazingly all this travelling had cost us only £4 each thanks to a "Mad March" scheme. An effort to play the Shrews four days later was also postponed.

The following week we demolished Birmingham 6-0, our biggest home league win for 19 years. Williams was sent off for two rough challenges on Wright, then we scored four in eleven minutes. We even missed a penalty and had one disallowed. John Bond's team were destroyed. There was a great feeling of positivity after this, the merger to most people's relief was off and the team had produced a performance full of flair and energy.

I wasn't intending to go to Sheffield on the following Tuesday night but after that win Jay convinced me it was a good idea. I met my Dad, working in London, for lunch and then got the train from St Pancras and had a good few beers in the Norfolk Arms near Bramall Lane. It was still "Mad March" so just a £4 fare. We didn't find a B&B for the night, but Jay said he knew of a train that ran which we would have time to catch after the game. We lost to a harsh penalty, with Wood having already saved one, in a game that we dominated for large parts. Coppell was not happy "George felt the forward conned the ref." We headed back to the station and found Jay's train did give us enough time, indeed it didn't leave until 23.55! Therefore, there was nothing for it but to head back to the Norfolk Arms. The train turned out to be the mail train that took over five hours to get back to London and was very cold. Jay slept the whole way. We arrived at St Pancras well before the tube had opened and got home at 7.30. I could have met Dad for breakfast.

The following day we signed midfielder Alan Pardew, a glazier, from Yeovil for £7,000. Meanwhile Noades thought the club could face closure, as four houses were to be built just 65 feet from the Old Stand. Ron was concerned they would object to the late alcohol licence the club enjoyed which could "destroy our livelihood".

We won with a dodgy late penalty put away from Gray with great power to keep the play-off hopes alive against Leeds. I had a letter printed in the Advertiser saying how Gray must stay so was glad he tucked it away as Paul feared I had jinxed it.

On a very wet night I got the coach to the rearranged Shrewsbury away game listening to my new personal cassette player and reading "Coach 1 News". The deluge that greeted us was so bad that a programme seller sold his wares on the coach so he, and our purchase, stayed dry. It began to dawn on us that the weather may well result in another postponement which, after a four-and-a-half-hour trip up, we dreaded. Only 2,555 hardy people saw the game that was a farce on a waterlogged pitch. We all reckoned Palace implored the ref, ironically a Mr Flood, not to call it off and avoid a fourth trip. I won a fiver on one of Joyce's lottery tickets, I used that to sit in the stand thinking it would be drier. Wrong. The wind just blew rain into me. It ended 0-0.

Millwall away was never a game anyone relished. Jay and I got the coach from Selhurst which took nearly two hours but avoided the dodgy walk to the ground. We nicked the game 1-0 with an early goal from Bright taking advantage of keeper Horne's blunder. Wood was as solid as ever in goal and we kept up our play-off hopes. We met a couple of Jay's mates at Victoria after the game, even though they were Brighton fans.

Jay, Paul, and I joined the usual couple of hundred making their way to Grimsby via Newark. These supporters' trains felt like a private club, you knew by sight just about everyone on them. Jay brought a pie, but his face told me it was grim. He turned to a policeman with a dog and said "mate, wanna give this to your friend – all its good for." We won, with Bright again grabbing the winner which I enjoyed too much twisting my ankle in the goal celebration in the handful of seats at the back of the terrace. A great three points considering Gray was sent off in the first half.

We had two disappointing home draws against Plymouth and WBA before we headed down to struggling Brighton on Easter Monday. I was picked up by the Brighton fans we met post

Millwall with Jay and we had a couple of drinks in the town centre before watching our powder puff display in a 2-0 defeat. We just can't win at this place. Paul left a little early to avoid the crowd and any trouble, but it didn't quite work out as minutes later we saw him being chased in the park behind our corner terrace. We resurrected our play-off hopes beating Oldham 2-1 thanks to early goals from Wright, and Bright who described his as "the best fluke I've scored".

Clubby still hadn't seen us win away so when he booked on my coach to Sunderland I feared the worst. It was a near six-hour journey but was pretty comfortable with most people having two seats to themselves and a variety of videos to enjoy including the latest "That's what I call music 9". We had little to cheer as an early deflected goal saw us lose 1-0 and left us three points adrift of the play-offs.

Pompey brought a huge travelling support to Selhurst having the Holmesdale and half the seats in the Arthur Wait. Chants of "going up" went on and on as did the annoying bell ringing fella but we spoilt the party big time with a late goal from Wright. It was sad and amusing at the same time to see former Palace favourite Hilaire sent off for a shove on Gray during some time-wasting antics. The mass ranks of Pompey fans were not happy, and a pitch invasion seemed inevitable at the end. Referee Hamer waited until he was close to the tunnel then blew up and ran. We decided to leg it to the station furthest from the Pompey fans, Thornton Heath, then to a few pubs in Croydon.

Paul drove up to our last match at Hull. We needed to win and hope Ipswich didn't to make the play-offs. We got there in good time so all of us, including Paul, had a more than a few pints in Hull town centre. The small away end was packed and expectant but Hull, with Alex Dyer outstanding, won 3-0. We were never in the game. Paul drove home, we didn't even think that he had been heavily drinking a few hours earlier.

Jim Canon was my player of the season and was ever present, as was George Wood, with Wright topping the scorers list.

We all thought it a good season. The question was could we make the jump from being on the verge of the play-offs and get back to the first division and if so what needed to improve. In Bright and Wright we had excellent strikers, Salako in his early games was looking promising on the wing and defensively we were generally sound. We liked Kevin Taylor but maybe it was the midfield that needed an upgrade.

Above – Kevin Mabbutt gets the winner at Leicester in 1982, a very rare away victory in our dark days.

Below - Chris Jones had a great debut against Wolves in 1982 but, as many of our strikers did in the early eighties, struggled.

Above – We had to win to stay up, not go up, against Burnley in 1983. Ian Edwards got the vital winner.

Below – Gavin Nebbeling in the shocking 5-0 home thrashing to Wimbledon in 1985. We were destroyed that day.

Above – Fortunes were starting to change, Ian Wright scores in a cracking 3-3 draw against Ipswich in 1986.

Below. In 1987 there was speculation the club would merge with Wimbledon and even Charlton. Not a popular prospect.

Above – Alan Irvine at Hull in 1987 when we came close to the play-offs. Below – The "disgrace" Eric Nixon is sent off in a dramatic second half at Maine Road in 1987.

Above – Bright scores at Blackburn in 1988, a mad game we lost 5-4. Below - The fourth penalty against Brighton in 1989 from Pemberton was blasted halfway up the Holmesdale

Pardew, Wright, and Bright celebrate our 1989 play-off semi-final victory. The drama against Blackburn awaited us.

Above - Eddie's late strike at Blackburn in the 1989 play offs caused mayhem on the away terrace…then we looked up.

Below – We were six down but this penalty could have got us back in the game in the 9-0 Anfield defeat in 1989…..!

Above - A cracking derby with Millwall in 1989, Wright put us ahead but Bright got the winner in a classic 4-3 win.

All photographs by Neil Everett.

Chapter 7: 1987/88 – Getting closer to the promised land.

The summer did not start too promisingly.

It was hoped that we could build on our improving team with some new signings. Instead, we heard that the hugely promising Andy Gray had rejected a new deal as had the hard-working Kevin Taylor and Gary Stebbing. With funds limited, and uncertainly over reliable keeper George Wood, there wasn't a lot of positive news around in May.

Our mood was boosted by the signing of Geoff Thomas, a versatile defensive midfielder from Crewe for £50,000 with former Palace manager Dario Gradi expressing his disappointment at losing his player of last season. That news was countered by Alan Irvine, a valued winger, leaving to join Dundee United for £55,000. He was then replaced in the squad by Neal Redfearn of Doncaster where he won their player of the season last year, and whose form had led to some interest from first division clubs.

Andy Gray and George Wood signed new contracts in July which was great news. But we promptly lost a player heavily criticised by my cousin Graham, Steve Ketteridge, to Orient. Andy Higginbottom, Brian Sparrow, and Anton Otulakowski were all given free transfers. The later the biggest loss despite his injury concerns, he eventually became manager of Hastings United during the season.

Pre-season saw a trip to Sweden and a procession of convincing victories against teams of dubious quality. Long serving groundsman Len Chatterton had a testimonial, a weird five a side involving no goalkeepers with teams of former players preceding a 2-1 defeat to Watford when we showed off a kit change, reverting to the red and blue stripes. That week we also signed a sponsorship deal, £200,00 with Andrew Copeland insurance.

I had reasonable confidence for the coming season and had a lengthy chat with my West Ham supporting mate Andy during a typical evening out in Brighton just before the season. This started with a few pints outside the station then a trip to Swifts for some deadly "between the sheets" cocktails where we agreed our bet of who would finish higher in their respective league. We progressed to the Top Rank nightclub opposite, and Andy realised I would happily increase the bet the more I drank. I began to have my suspicions that Andy had spiked my drinks a little as my gin and tonics were a mysterious colour. I wasn't that bothered until I woke up in the morning to my Mum's Rod Stewart tape seemingly at full volume.

The first game was at Huddersfield. I drove and picked up Paul in Oxted then to Tadworth to pick up James aka Clubby where there was no answer to our door banging. We threw stones at his window, shouted, and hooted the horn. Nothing. How long should we wait? No mobiles to ring in those days. Eventually he appeared, hungover, and off we went, with me a little nervous that some of Clubby's symptoms may affect the inside of my car. I hadn't seen Palace win in any of the six games I had driven to, but it was looking good after half time. Bright scored two crackers, one from 20 yards the other a neat chip. It didn't last. Annoying Trevitt pulled one back, a goal with a hint of offside about it, and we then conceded a last gasp equaliser. As my Dad would say a point away is a point gained so we headed back down the M1 feeling cheerful enough.

The first home game started with disaster, two down in five minutes against Hull meant early season hope was dented. Referee Kelvin Morton came to the rescue giving us two second half penalties inevitably buried by Gray, the second won by Wright whose pace was a constant threat.

I went to a distant family wedding the following Saturday. I had no idea who the happy couple were but nevertheless I had to miss Barnsley away. We lost to a last-minute goal. Coppell was unimpressed "No brain, lung or leg power." Our form didn't improve at home to impressive Middlesbrough, but we did win 3-1 with two late goals from Bright including one which was suspiciously offside according to Coppell. Oh well, three points!

The start to the season had been disappointing, and Clubby still hadn't seen Palace win an away match so when he joined us in the car the prospects seemed bleak for a trip to Birmingham City. We took our place in the big, covered terrace to the side of the goal and saw Bright score yet again at the far end with a close-range header from Salako's cross to put us ahead at half time. Nobody could have predicted what would happen in the second half. We scored five more and totally demolished Birmingham, who included future West Ham and Liverpool full back Julian Dicks, who couldn't cope with the pace of Wright, power of Gray, and class of Bright. "What a load of rubbish" the home fans jeered from a deserted huge terrace. It was an eye-catching result that would have shown the rest of the division we were a team to take note of. The game was covered by Birmingham's club video and many copies were ordered from South London, including by me. Clubby's jinx had ended in style with a win that matched a record that had stood for 52 years, which I celebrated by stopping the car on the hard shoulder, getting out, and punching the air to some bemused looks from other cars.

With new signings Thomas and Redfearn getting stronger we then thrashed Ron Atkinson's WBA 4-1. We had kept the same eleven for the first six games – Wood, Stebbing, Brush, Gray, Nebbeling, Cannon, Redfearn, Thomas, Bright, Wright and Salako. That was broken up against Leicester with O'Reilly replacing the injured Stebbing but Jay, my Dad and I saw Wright score again in a 2-1 win to put us top of the league! We were in dominating form and for the first-time promotion started to seem like when and not if with Mark Bright and Ian Wright becoming a formidable partnership. Ian was full of praise the more experienced players "I've a lot to thank Mark Bright and Jimmy Cannon for, they are the ones who give me stick when I do the wrong thing and make me work harder".

Having endured the night train last season, Paul thankfully drove to Sheffield United for the Tuesday evening game. Wright put the league leaders ahead but we couldn't hold on, not least as the ref seemed obsessed with giving all decisions to the home team.

We were certainly capable of periods of brilliance that could blow teams away at this stage but could look dodgy at the back. This was true at Reading. After being a goal down at half time we produced three goals in twelve minutes and the game was won. We were second and hopes were very high on the way back down the M4, some friends had an accident on the way up so that prompted a more cautious drive. We were just worried about the speculation that Mark Bright was subject of a bid of £450,000 from Watford. Happily Palace, despite not being flush, made it clear promotion not selling was the priority. However, Bright's absence from a 4-0 thrashing of Newport in the League cup set tongues wagging. Not least on the way home when Andy quipped "We may take Bright as a reserve at West Ham. Petty cash mate"

Hopes were high for the Ipswich home game. Second in the league and scoring stacks of goals encouraged nearly 11,000 to show up, a marked improvement helped by the relaunched "Bring a Pal to the Palace" campaign. Typically, we didn't perform though. Ipswich looked stronger throughout with Jason Dozzell outstanding and they won 2-1.

Our previous optimism was dented with Andy Gray sounding unsettled with depressing rumours of a move to Villa "I think a fresh challenge would do me good" he said on Clubcall (0898 121145), a premium rate phone number that had content that changed daily. I used to call it every day working at TACA whilst eating crisps from our sandwich man. Andy and I would also phone the oppositions clubcall to find out if they had terrible injuries. Some days we even did some work.

Life at TACA now included breaks for over two hours twice a week to play a variety of sports from basketball to trampolining. Sometimes a drink in the Sun was called for as well as all that exercise makes you thirsty, or in need of a Cornish Pasty and Chips. We remained overpaid and underworked, and importantly getting time off to follow Palace was never a problem.

Our convoluted trip to Shrewsbury via the M1, M6, M54, A5 plus a terrible pub selling terrible food with terrible service, "go somewhere else if it's not to your posh London standards" didn't go well. We lost 2-0 with the inexperienced Richard Shaw struggling at full back. My bigger concern was the potential departure of Gray as I was sure if we kept our team together, we would be close to automatic promotion this season.

We beat Newport 2-0 in the second leg of the league cup to go through 6-0 on aggregate, I was able to poke fun at Andy as they lost 5-2 to Barnsley. However, the Gray situation came to a head the next day. He would be on the transfer list for 28 days, with the proviso that he would come off it should no club meet our valuation. I was keeping my fingers crossed that nobody came up with the £500k. At least we improved our squad by signing experienced left back David Burke from Huddersfield for £78,000.

Millwall were very impressive against us the following week. I went in the Old Stand thinking that was the safest bet and was joined by Clubby, Paul and Steve Robson. We watched Terry Hurlock control the midfield and with Sheringham and Cascarino very dangerous they were the only team who looked likely to score. Thankfully they didn't, Bright got a winner against the run of play, and we beat a hasty retreat to Croydon as there were outbreaks of crowd trouble all over the place which even led to an apology to supporters in a future home programme. Bright was proving a very astute buy.

On Friday 16th October we were due to be playing Oldham away. On the previous night I had been at Crawley College and came out about 9pm and thought it was a little breezy. The next morning I woke up at 7am having not seen any of the destructive hurricane that swept across the south east of England. Trees were covering our road, the garden was a shambles, and it was hard just to walk into work in the morning. I wasn't all that bothered about that. The bigger issue is how do I get to Oldham this evening? I walked home at lunchtime and managed to drive as far as Clubby's Tadworth house when we found out that the game was off – the wind had made the roof of a stand too dangerous. Oh well, beer and snooker evening then.

Our evening train trip to Villa was fruitless. A 4-1 defeat despite looking decent for long stretches of the game, but a failing offside trap didn't help. A pub with a pool table in a pub near Witton station was a rare highlight.

If the prospect of losing Gray was worrying it sounded as if Coppell was unsettled too, with the Sun quoting our manager as saying, "I'll see out my contract to the end of the season and take it from there, I don't think I'll sign another here" and "I hate being the boss." Not ideal, particularly as we were up there with the best in the division. I was frustrated and the need to get promotion was suddenly more urgent before we lost our manager and key players. At least Coppell was quick to say his comments had been taken out of context. It didn't seem to affect us as we beat Swindon 2-1.

Our potential would be truly tested by a trip to Manchester United in the League cup third round. Young full-back Mark Hone had been struggling and this was a tough night for him as McClair got a penalty, and a second within 25 minutes. We made a game of it though when obscure Irish defender O'Doherty pulled one back and we held our own after that.

A defeat at Bradford had left us in 8th, but we found form with a fantastic performance at home to Plymouth winning 5-1. Andy Gray was magnificent in midfield, Burke overlapped superbly, and Wright was looking too good for this division. I was pleased to see Nebbeling get the fifth; he had got a nasty head injury at Old Trafford but had kept playing anyway. Andy came along and said, "we could be playing you next season". He rarely offered us much praise so that did leave me thinking we could do it this year.

Bournemouth away was fun. We were two down in twelve minutes and the Palace end was less than happy. By half time we were 3-2 up and should have added more in the second. A sour note at Bournemouth was the treatment of Palace fans by the police. There seemed to be arbitrary arrests and unprovoked attacks. Complaints were made by supporters, and by the Club, with Noades writing to both Bournemouth police and the football league. There was no doubt that football supporters were regularly treated very badly across the country, we were often frogmarched through towns by the police and threatened with arrest if you broke away. No other law-abiding people in the country were treated in this way and it was resented. South Yorkshire and the West Midland forces had the worst reputation with most supporters. Travelling supporters were often made as unwelcome by the police as they were by the opposition fans. There was no doubt this situation began to change after each disaster of the 1980's starting with the Bradford fire in 1985. The general feeling was the police would always be supported by the authorities and so could act with impunity at grounds in arresting or intimidating people who were just travelling and following their team, often in decaying grounds, with zero interest in any fighting. There were some policemen that came from the Palace area and knew us and that was a saving grace sometimes, together with stewards at some grounds who were "proper" supporters themselves. Some stewards weren't too great though and at Bournemouth some were very inflammatory. In his honest "direct view" programme article director Geoff Geraghty was appalled saying those stewards could have caused a nasty situation.

The Gray saga was continuing. Noades was accusing Villa of dirty tactics in making an undervalued offer to unsettle a key player of a rival. They wanted to pay £150,000. Palace wanted £500,000. Coppell said he would love Gray to stay, so would I. Possible replacements were reportedly Kevin Langley and John Bumstead. Neither sounded like they could fill Gray's shoes. Jim Cannon waded into the debate telling anyone wanting to leave to "grow up and shut up as Palace are going places".

I decided to miss our debut in the Simod Cup to play in a pool match for the Moonraker pub in Crawley. Just 1,400 saw Palace lose 1-0 at first division Oxford on a wet cold night.

No such cold weather for me to endure against Stoke. I won a director's box ticket thanks to the lifeline draw. Andy and I enjoyed a generous lunch in the John Wilson Executive Lounge with never ending champagne with comic Barry Williams entertainingly poking fun at everyone. For this reason Andy was keen I didn't tell him he supported West Ham. My secrecy cost him a few rounds in Croydon after the game. We sat behind Noades and I celebrated a 2-0 win to take us up to 5th.

Gray didn't play against Stoke. There had been a row between him and Coppell and he left to join Villa for £150,000. It was very disappointing. It seemed a glazier, Alan Pardew, could be his replacement. That didn't seem likely to enhance our chances of promotion.

After many road trips this season, Jay, Paul, Clubby and Jay Thayre and I got the club special train to Blackburn, trying and failing not to laugh at the train spotters. They stood in the cold jotting numbers down for some reason as we changed at Crewe for Mill Hill. A good card session for me, with Jay and I taking money off Paul, who was devastated at losing at least £1.25 to the amusement of the rest of us. The game was poor. Wright and Bright had an off day, and the defence wasn't good enough to grind out a point and we lost 2-0, plus O'Doherty was sent off. The highlight of the two hours on the terrace behind a big fence was the splendid meat and potato pies with, glory be, sachets of HP sauce available.

One friend who didn't go was Trevor Fitsall. He had started playing in our five a side team and he had a stinging letter published in the Croydon Advertiser slating Gray for leaving. Coppell replaced Gray with Glenn Pennyfather for £150,000 from Southend and picked up Dennis Bailey a non-league forward.

Pennyfather didn't play in the 3-0 win over Leeds which cheered a dreary day. Cannon had missed a couple of games and his presence always made us look far more solid. Ian Wright, who was looking quicker in every game he played, scored yet again.

Next up Manchester City away, who also expected to be in the promotion mix come May. The first half was dull. The second half wasn't. City took the lead with the much-heralded Paul Lake dashing through our defence to score on 68 minutes. Then four minutes later came the drama. Just after City keeper Nixon had been booked for a scuffle with Bright, the two met again on the penalty spot with our striker trying to make his drop kick awkward. Nixon then punched him right in front of the Palace end. Our supporters were infuriated, and all manner of ferocious abuse was hurled at Nixon. Weirdly the most memorable came from me and all I said was "You're a disgrace number one" Luckily the referee didn't buckle in front of the big home crowd and sent Nixon off. "Hey, it must be a penalty too" I said to Jay and Vince Nemenyi nodded, "They'll go fuckin' loopy over there if he gives it." He gave the penalty.

They did go loopy. We equalised with Redfearn staying calm in the heat of it all having replaced the departed Gray as penalty taker. City had lost their heads and some awful tackles came flying in, but we realised we had a chance to win this and Bright, centre of all the booing from the Kippax end, scored twice to give us a 3-1 lead. The ref did give City a dodgy penalty, missed by Paul Stewart, which would have made it 2-2. Luckily, the police did us a favour and kept us in the ground for over half an hour with hundreds of City fans not exactly wishing us a safe journey home whilst bashing on the exit doors. Noades didn't calm the waters behind the scenes saying, "City couldn't handle defeat " whilst referee Deakin was having stitches after being hit by a coin. Just two days before my 21st it was a great afternoon, and we enjoyed many a beer on the way home as we moved up to 4th.

That impressive win was followed by another characterful performance at home to Sheffield United, trailing at half time we scored a controversial retaken penalty, didn't get another when Wright was brought down, but the busy Barber got a winner anyway. Jay, Paul, and I then travelled to Hull on the club train, with all traditions in place – the squeaky refreshment trolley, card games and predictascore but despite a decent performance we lost to goals from Garry Parker and Alex Dyer. The game saw Pennyfather's debut, he looked useful and the expectation was he would replace Pardew.

Having lost Gray there was rumours around that Watford wanted Ian Wright, but a bid of £450,000 was rejected. I was pleased about that, and of the snooker hall that was planned to open on top of Sainsbury's offering hope of a few frames after home games. Sadly, it never materialised.

Boxing Day was a tough one, Ipswich away. I was enjoying our traditional family day in Hastings with the usual buffet, pontoon, and gin, but the earlier walk around Alexandra Park was ruined when I heard we were a goal down after four minutes. My heart jumped a beat though when my grandad put final score on. My eyes shot halfway down the screen "Ipswich 2-3 C.Palace". Yes please to that gin!

The next day - yes, the next day, with no whining about tiredness we lost 3-2 to Reading where our defence struggled with the pace of Michael Gilkes. A shame as the crowd had jumped up to 12,500.

Now into 1988 there was no doubt we were improving. The pace and power we had in the team was a stark contrast to a few years ago. During 1987 Bright and Wright had scored 43 goals and had just about played every game with only George Wood appearing more. Crowds were rising at long last too, by over 20% compared to 1986.

The Barnsley home game on New Year's Day summed us up. Lively going forward but iffy at the back; but we did win 3-2. The next day (again) we travelled to Leicester who couldn't cope with Wright in the first half as we scored four by half time to lead 4-2 over the tea and Mars bars. Then our very shaky defence let us down and we ended up drawing 4-4. Leicester's third came from a loose ball wide of the penalty area on our right that Wood should have kicked into the stand, but instead tried to find a pass to Pennyfather, and Reid nipped in to score into an empty net. It was to be the beginning of the end for Wood's highly consistent spell as our keeper who admitted he wasn't enjoying his football and wanted a change.

Wood played his last game at first division Newcastle in the FA Cup. I had a long 650-mile round trip on the club coach which left at 7.10 and arrived at 2.15 including a stop at the nearby Board Inn which was better than being in the freezing ground for any longer than necessary. I stood at the front corner of the terrace, and like everyone thought the ground looked bigger on TV. The game is remembered for a spectacular winner from young Paul Gascoigne which beat Wood from 30 yards. Pardew did have a goal disallowed for an alleged push and we were unlucky not to nick a draw with Redfearn having one of his best games since joining us.

Wood sadly left for Cardiff and was replaced by Perry Suckling, signed for £100,000 from Manchester City. Suckling made his debut against Huddersfield who we beat, unconvincingly, 2-1 and were up to second with a game in hand but three points behind Andy Gray's Villa. The top two go up automatically (with the next three going in the play offs), and we were now favourites for one of those two spots. My god we have made some progress over the last few years, plus we have £200,000 available for further new signings thanks to the Lifeline scheme.

After Newcastle Paul and I had another long coach trip, this time to Middlesbrough. A cold 8am departure for a six-hour journey to arrive onto an icy pavement and a blistering wind. At least we were under cover in the £4 seats behind the goal, but the roof gave no respite against the Arctic wind. Our shivering got worse as we missed first half chances and lost 2-1.

On the following Friday night Paul drove up to Oldham. We hadn't scored in our previous four games on plastic pitches and sadly this was no different, and when Tommy Wright scored for them that was that. We also had a little parking incident. Paul was determined to find some free street parking, but Jay and I were pressurising him to hurry up as we were desperate to get out the car and find a toilet, one of the pitfalls of in car drinking. We finally found a residential street and as Paul manipulated his splendidly hardworking Fiesta into a tight spot, he very gently knocked a small garden wall which must have been weak to say the least. No damage to the car, but the entire little wall immediately collapsed. Paul beat a hasty retreat as curtains twitched. These night games were tiring, and we had managed three massive trips in January. This time I arrived home at 4am.

The following day I went with Andy to see West Ham at QPR in the FA Cup, still dozy from the previous night in Oldham. There were a ridiculous number of Hammers fans trying to get into the away end and many overflowed on to the pitch which meant the game was held up for ages. This was not good news. We were on a tight schedule to get back to Crawley for a Jimmy Jones comedy gig. We nearly missed the train too as Andy dropped his programme, that always had to be in mint condition, into a puddle of beer. West Ham lost 3-1, but the gig was great if not entirely politically correct.

Defeat at Oldham meant that we had completed the 15 games which were a league within a league. The top four from our division in this alternative league decided qualifying for the Mercantile Credit Football Festival at Wembley. We made it, just. In April we sat through seemingly never ending 30-minute matches, rarely with any goals, from 10am until we played at 5.30 against Sheffield Wednesday which we lost on penalties when Phil Barber missed. Palace sold 6,000 tickets for a tedious day poorly attended which will surely never be repeated. It was not the way to see your club at Wembley for the first time.

I went on my first lads' holiday with Andy to Tenerife in February. We had a great time, and it was the first of a stack of fabulous trips across the world. This included a day in a waterpark, getting the hotel coach there but missing the return trip as we couldn't resist more goes on the massive kamikaze slide. There were no taxis, so we faced a 6-mile hike back to the hotel with Andy struggling after eating a hot dog of dubious quality which had the expected effect! We stopped off at a bar where I found out we had beat Birmingham 3-0. That gave me the energy for the last mile. Andy was in a state of shock after hearing of West Ham's draw at mighty Liverpool.

From the sun of Tenerife to the glamour of a 1-0 defeat at West Bromwich. We looked the better team, but our forwards let us down for once. I had travelled up by train and was getting a lift back from Paul. However, we got separated in the crowd leaving the ground and I couldn't find them anywhere. No mobiles of course! I only had a single train ticket and didn't think I had enough cash on me for a return trip, it was also raining and cold and I wasn't sure what to do. I walked round the ground in the hope of luckily bumping into Paul but no joy. But I did see John Salako outside the main entrance. I plucked up the courage and said to John "Would there be any chance of a lift back on the team coach?" and explained the situation "You better check with the boss, but I'm sure it'll be OK – we've done that before". Great, I thought. Then Paul drove past the ground, waved at me and my trip on the team coach was off, so I thanked John and off I went.

The following week I went with Andy and his Man United supporting mate Paul Lewis to see them play at Arsenal thinking it'll be interesting to see what the first division is like again in case we did make it. It was pretty daunting. Both teams looked so good in front of 54,000. Arsenal won 2-1 with McClair missing a late penalty for United. We then hit the Allsop Arms in Baker Street and had another cracking night out. It was great in those days when you could just decide to go to a game like that on the spur of the moment. I so wanted to join Paul and Andy in the first division club but on the way out of Highbury Eighth Wonders "I'm not scared" was on the PA. I did feel a little scared for us if we did go up, but it would be so exciting if we did.

Shrewsbury at home. Lost to a late goal. Terrible performance. "God, I hate Shrewsbury," said Paul. Didn't we all, they were such a bogey team to us. The best bit was a few beers in Crystals with comic Barry Williams on fine form. This gloomy afternoon didn't prevent Palace signing a £250,000 sponsorship deal with Virgin Atlantic. It needed delicate negotiation with the less high-profile Andrew Copeland over the more modest deal signed earlier in the season. It was sealed with Virgin bigwigs attending a far better performance in a 3-1 win over Oldham, who struggled to cope with our grass pitch. The game also marked ever reliable Jim Cannon's 650th match.

Supporting West Ham Andy didn't like Millwall much so joined us on the club coach which left from Fairfield Hall as rumours had existed of a Millwall ambush if they left from Selhurst. We stood on the corner terrace and for a few minutes I read the programme. When I looked up as the teams came out, I realised I couldn't read the advertising boards at the far end. It turned out I needed contact lenses. Like many I was working more with fledgling computers now and they got the blame. Sheringham put Millwall ahead and we weren't playing well, but a late scramble at the far end, that I struggled to see, ended with pandemonium around me as Cannon bundled in an equaliser off his thigh (or hand?) and we were only two points outside the play-offs. We got back on our coach and we were pleased we didn't have to face the angry Millwall fans in the streets. Eight years later we beat them 4-1, and on the way back to the station we were described as "fodder" with middle aged men running around with knives. I doubt the trip back to New Cross Gate for those on the train was much better than that after this late equaliser.

A dull draw with Bradford was followed by a trip to roundabout ridden Swindon which was never an easy place to go but had a decent atmosphere. I travelled up with Vince and when Wright and Bright put us 2-1 up we thought we had the points, but a late goal went against us this time and meant we settled for an archbishop.

Bournemouth arrived on 2nd April, and we had our old friend Kelvin Morton as ref. He gave us two first half penalties, and insisted that one which was saved was retaken, Redfearn despatched both. He did send off Ian Wright too for retaliating with a lunge at Mark Newsom. Bright sealed it with a third and looked classes better than our former striker Aylott playing for Bournemouth. Big Trev got some stick from the crowd but joked with Cannon that "I got worse when I played for Palace". We were 5th and in the play-off places.

Transfer deadline day passed with one signing, right back John Pemberton coming in from Crewe, possibly on the advice of former teammate Geoff Thomas.

We got a draw at Stoke, or I think we did. It was a terrible low view through a big fence. Next we welcomed Andy Gray back to Selhurst with Villa, it was a feisty atmosphere so much so that my Dad got a police warning! It was our biggest crowd of the season, 16.476, and it looked like Platt's goal was winning it for them until Gray lunged in on Wright and who scored the resulting late penalty for a draw. As I had an expensive start to 1988 I gave Plymouth away a miss where we won 3-1.

The season ticket prices for next season were out and I was disappointed that lifeline members only got a 10% discount. I wrote to the club about it but got a very reasonable letter back from Ron Noades explaining why he didn't wish to accept my offer of paying £60 rather than £72 for the Arthur Wait Enclosure.

I won another lifeline prize, which made my moan about my season tickets seem harsh! This time I had a choice of various items, but I was always unlikely to select the kettle, iron, or blank video tapes. Instead, I chose lunch for two and seats in an executive box for the Blackburn home game. This time I went with Dad and we had a great meal and, although the box was comfortable, we both preferred being in the stand rather than behind the window. We saw Suckling save a penalty from Archibald, before Bright and Thomas got us the points.

Our last away game was at Leeds. We desperately needed a result to get in the top five before the last round of games. It just didn't work out though. Despite optimism created by a nine-game unbeaten run during a snooker session at Clubby's house we lost to a first half penalty. This meant we had to beat

Manchester City at home then hope already promoted Millwall did not lose to Blackburn to get in the play offs.

In the days before mobiles it was people with ears to radios that drew the most attention. It was goalless at half time but the gloomy news from Millwall was that Blackburn were winning 2-0. However, rumours circulated that Millwall had fought back and it was now 3-3. Nobody was sure if this was true. Then Nebbeling scored, and the play-offs seemed on, even more so when Thomas got a second to put us two up as City wilted. Just as the excitement reached fever pitch I found out, overhearing a radio, that Blackburn had won 4-1. No play-offs then. Nevertheless, there were hundreds of people over the advertising boards by now and the inevitable pitch invasion arrived when the ref brought our season to an end in the warm sunshine.

We had finished 6th. One place outside the play-offs. So close but yet so far.

Andy Gray did get promotion with Villa. They finished just three points ahead of us and it was reasonable to assume that had he have stayed we would have made it to the first division.

Despite that it had been a cracking season. The two key signings last summer were a success, Redfearn heading the appearance list followed by Thomas, who won my player of the season. We had the league's top scorers in Bright and Wright who had 49 between them, and the best home record. If we could keep our top players, then surely we would do even better next season. But it was the "if" in that sentence that was the worry. Surely other clubs would be trying to take our strikers off us and if we did keep them, we surely had to get promoted next season to hold on to them.

The defence did need some work, so I was shocked when Jim Cannon was released. It was hard to imagine him not running out next season. It was also a crying shame we didn't know this before his last game so that he got the send-off he so richly deserved. There were reports that there was a rift between the younger players and the old guard over recent years, with the likes of Cannon and Wood who were so crucial to keeping us in the division in prior seasons not always appreciating the approach of the younger brigade such as Wright, Gray and Finnigan. At least Cannon had a good testimonial earlier in the season, a fun 3-3 draw with Spurs featuring Swindlehurst and Burridge and an impressive Coppell on the wing.

.

Chapter 8: 1988/89 – Now or never

I breathed a big sigh of relief in August.

We still had our two deadly strikers, Ian Wright, and Mark Bright not to mention Geoff Thomas in midfield. This meant we were certainly going to be among the favourites for promotion come May. We lost a few players who were not A-listers. O'Doherty to Huddersfield for £25,000, more disappointingly Tony Finnigan to Blackburn for £45,000, and Gary Stebbing joined KV Oostende in Belgium.

We were linked with a trio of players from our 1979 team over the summer - Nicholas, Sansom and Hilaire. Nicholas did train with us for a bit but ended up joining Chelsea and Sansom was above our budget.

We did sign a reserve keeper, Brian Parkin from Crewe for a nominal fee, then two free transfers - midfielder Dave Madden from Reading and striker Steve Claridge from Weymouth. The big summer signing had to be a defender as Cannon had left so a replacement for him was essential. A tribunal decided that we should pay Fulham £240,000 for Jeff Hopkins who would presumably partner fit again Gary O'Reilly, or Gavin Nebbeling who had been named club captain. Geoff Thomas was the obvious candidate to take over from Cannon as Team Captain.

There were a couple of other football stories over the summer. Firstly, yet another bid by the top clubs in the first division to breakaway and sell their rights separately to TV and make the league a closed shop with no promotion. That didn't sound attractive to me and not in the spirit of sport at all. Secondly there was a bidding war for live league coverage which was eventually won by ITV who beat the BBC and a fledging satellite company. Football still had a terrible reputation thanks to hooliganism and decaying grounds, and there were still some who wanted it banned!

Andy Gray caused another rumpus claiming, "Palace treated me like dirt" and "It was so disorganised with Mr Palace, Jim Cannon, ruling the roost." Our chairman Ron Noades dismissed the claims as "a pack of lies" and went on to say the club was on a far stronger financial footing at long last and described this stable situation as a "bloody miracle". There was no doubt that the lifeline scheme had been a great success and was making a significant impact.

Pre-season friendlies saw another Swedish tour followed by a win at Crewe arranged as part of a deal to take their keeper Brian Parkin as backup. I saw all the usual faces at Fulham for a comfortable win but had to find cover from a torrential downpour under a thin advertising board. Fulham kindly opened the stand for us eventually. We decided to give our win at Millwall a miss feeling it was wise to keep trips there to a minimum.

Our first game at Swindon was postponed, as their ground was unsafe, I thought the game should have been switched to Selhurst. Instead of Swindon Andy and I stayed in Southampton and saw his West Ham boys get slaughtered on a baking day 4-0. The Hammers efforts on the pitch made it seem as if their players were as massively pissed as seemingly all their fans were. We stayed in a very dodgy £7 B&B where there were two pots of paint in our room and a dirty motorbike so Alex Polizzi would have had plenty to say.

We kicked off, with John Henty back doing the PA, against Chelsea under the lights. It was real blood and thunder stuff. Thomas was outstanding and a draw was a fair result, I was relieved with that as Durie missed a penalty for them. On the Saturday we failed to score for the first time at home in 27 games in a very disappointing 2-0 defeat to impressive Watford.

I didn't go to the 0-0 at Walsall as West Ham Andy, friend Paul Lewis and I were flying to Corfu that evening. Instead, I went with Andy to see his Hammers win at Wimbledon before heading to Gatwick. We had a great time in Faliraki and the bars got heavily hit. One night, for reasons best known to me, I decided to jump fully dressed into a swimming pool outside one lively pub. Suddenly it seemed like quite a swim to the edge after plenty of gin and tonics. I walked back sodden, got changed, then went out again. Sunny days, water sports and boat trips made it a bundle of fun. One day had an air of disappointment as my massive radio cassette player, which just about picked up the world service on the beach, told me Palace had only drawn with Shrewsbury and the crowd had got frustrated. That was something for my cousin Graham to deal with as he had started 12 years of stewarding.

My Mum picked me up from Gatwick the morning after Palace played at Sunderland. Forget my good time, what was the score! "One all, O'Reilly scored for Palace" Mum said. We still hadn't won this season.

I drove to Portsmouth via James's house in Tadworth with Vince and Adrian. We were appalled at the £5 charged to stand on the uncovered terrace with no refreshments and dire toilet facilities. The miserable stewards wouldn't even let us put up a small flag. We went behind to a penalty, but Wright got us a draw. This season was not going well, somehow the team just wasn't clicking and we were five off bottom. The mood in the squad didn't seem great, so much so that Redfearn had put in a transfer request.

The click finally happened on 1st October against Plymouth. We thrashed them 4-1 and it looked like the shackles had been released. We hit the woodwork four times as well, and after the game I was impatient to get climbing back up the league. That form continued with a 2-0 win over Ipswich with Wright and Bright yet again scoring during an excellent first half performance to get us to midtable at least.

Fanzines were making a welcome appearance around now, and our excellent Eagle Eye was on its fourth issue. Up until then the only publications on sale were official club productions which could sound like propaganda. Now we had independent material which was not afraid to be sarcastic, critical, and funny and express how fans really felt about their club. An excellent book "Is that the Programme" by Chris Lehman tells their story very well during the 1990's.

Next was Blackburn away and an astonishing match. Clubby and I went up on the £13 club coach run by Adam Sells who carried out several club roles and treated us to a video of the Ipswich home game and "The Secret of my success". We got stand seats and saw us drawing 1-1 at half time with no great dramas. At the start of the second half we kicked on and Blackburn couldn't cope with Wright's pace as he added a second, then Bright a third and they looked a battered team. On yet another run past their demoralised defenders Wright was hacked down in the box for the most obvious penalty you could imagine. I swear referee Mr J.J. Timmons felt sorry for Rovers and didn't give it assuming, as we did, that we would score again soon enough anyway. That let-off seemed to inspire Blackburn and they then got a ridiculous penalty when O'Reilly tackled Scott Sellars as clean as you like but Mr Timmons decided this was the time to point to the spot. Coppell was furious and had to be restrained by the police. The papers described the penalty as "a gift". Rovers got two more to take the lead 4-3, as we sat back in our seats feeling robbed. Then O'Reilly popped up with a header to make it 4-4, but their talisman Colin Hendry got a last gasp winner, so we lost 5-4. There was many a heated debate on the way back with even the coach driver saying how terrible the ref was which probably increased his tip. We owed Blackburn one. Referee Mr J.J. Timmons was subject to ridicule in Eagle Eye including "he holds the record for a referee running 100 yards, a stunning 1 hour 23 minutes."

The victory over Swindon in the League cup seemed very dull by comparison a few days later, but the news that followed wasn't as Palace gave first division Sheffield Wednesday permission to talk to Coppell about their managerial vacancy. Luckily, that went no further.

After the Blackburn fiasco the trip to Bradford produced a much tighter display, and we defended Wright's goal very well. Another coach trip, this time with Trev's mate Rob Ellis who had appeared to cover for me as my bad back stopped me playing in goal in our five a side team. The problem was he played so well he held his place in our A team for the next sixteen years. Our one-off summer was clearly anything but and we were now playing all year round and doing well with our team made up of those going up and down the country with Palace, plus West Ham Andy. Some clubs even put in cash bids for our players, and we formed a 'B' team who were a little less successful.

Palace's upturn in form continued with a good win over Hull and we were now finally in the top half. Alex Dyer, as ever, looked good for Hull and the 3-1 score was harsh on them. Brian Parkin had been in goal for much of the season with Suckling injured but that apart our squad was looking in good shape. We won again against Oxford with a second half Redfearn penalty in a game we dominated, despite Wright being injured. Our ropy early season form was now becoming a distant memory. Crowds were continuing to rise, with over 10,000 seeing us rise to 5th.

It was back to the coach with Clubby and Adrian for the trip to Stoke, which didn't leave until 10.15 for some reason but we arrived just in time for kick off. The view was rubbish on the terrace, so we invested £6.50 for a seat but had sun in our eyes throughout a poor game losing 2-1. David Burke got injured and the lad behind us asked "Is Uncle David dead?" Let's hope not I thought. An excellent curry in Tadworth cheered things up. It was back on the coach for Bristol City in the League cup and what a disastrous trip it was. We were thrashed 4-1. The coach broke down on the Purley Way, so we missed the first half and had to listen to reports on Sport on Two which told us we were 3-0 down before even getting into the ground, for the oh so generous offer of the U16 price.

A forum with Noades and Coppell was held where subjects varied from a roof on the Holmesdale (cost somewhere way above £500k), possibility of seats above the terrace at the Sainsbury's end, and the need for any players signed to fit into our strict wage structure so team spirit is not damaged. It was an open and interesting meeting.

Barnsley came and showed their time-wasting skills to get a 1-1 draw with Coppell admitting "we didn't quite have the guile around the box." We were still missing the injured Wright.

The following week we added to our forward options by signing Alex Dyer for £225.000, who had always looked so impressive against us playing for Hull. I just hoped this wouldn't signal the departure of Redfearn who had Southampton sniffing around him. Dyer was on the bench at Bournemouth which was a dismal affair, Aylott scoring for them as they beat us 2-0. Coppell made the players sit through the video on Monday, some punishment that. Adrian and I had travelled in Clubby's car, but he did get a little lost and we ended up heading towards Reading at one point.

That week Redfearn left for Watford which was disappointing. He felt "there was no way I could patch up my differences as I have fallen out with the manager." At least the interest Wimbledon had in Wright was rebuffed, and rumours were dismissed that Manchester United and Everton were interested in Bright. Meanwhile reserve striker Steve Claridge left for Aldershot for £14,000, we would come across him many years later and not in a good way.

Feeling rough with a cold I made my way to Selhurst to see us beat Leicester 4-2, the three second half goals with Thomas outstanding in midfield made me feel much better so "Yes Andy, I am up for a beer and curry after the game".

Following a low key Simod Cup win over Walsall, Paul's trusty Fiesta made its merry way to WBA but the traffic was very bad, and we only just made kick off. The journey was not helped by a seemingly never-ending tape of Ned's Atomic Dustbins going full blast through dodgy back seat speakers where I was sitting with Robbie. We saw Alex Dyer get his first goal but defensively we were a shambles with Pennyfather struggling at left back and we lost 5-3. Very entertaining, but like the Blackburn game ultimately no points and we were now just in mid table.

During the week I went with Andy to see West Ham thrash Liverpool 4-1. They were excellent but they were also bottom of the first division. Wow, is that the standard? Going up suddenly looked full of stress! We made little progress towards promotion with a 0-0 draw with Manchester City. We had by far the better of the game but couldn't find a way past their keeper Dibble.

Meanwhile the government were looking to introduce a fan detested membership scheme for football supporters in a bid to counter hooliganism. The idea being if you caused trouble, according to the police, your card would be taken away and you couldn't go to any matches anywhere in the country. This would increase the power of the boys in blue over supporters further. Clubs were not happy. It took away the ability for spur of the moment decisions for people to go to matches who were not regular supporters. "It could lose us 3,000 fans" said Noades. There were many protests, with Palace gaining 4,000 signatures against it in a single home game. A few weeks ago, many fans were ejected from the Arthur Wait Enclosure for very minor "offences" that would have meant any membership card being revoked. Palace director Geoff Geraghty was doing his best to stand up for supporters in numerous meetings with South Norwood Police.

The usual crew joined me in my Vauxhall Cavalier which was very comfortable for away trips, but my chart-based tapes were not quite to the liking of Paul and Jay as we made our way to Birmingham. We won with a goal direct from Dyer's corner, but we kept playing the offside trap which made me very nervous.

We also won at Southampton in the Simod Cup with Dyer getting the winner, impressive as they were 6th in the first division. During half time the players were warned by the police that they faced arrest if they continued to swear as the crowd was so low they could hear all the shouting. Seemed harsh! A dull 0-0 with Leeds followed. The highlight was comic Barry Williams announcing a likely new signing in the bar before the game, Rudi Hedman, from Colchester for £40,000. "I bet Brian Clough's new signings aren't announced by a comedian at the City Ground," said Paul.

Brighton away on Boxing Day was like playing a bad film yet again. We lost 3-1 even though they were in the bottom three. That's seven successive defeats in that decaying ground. It was in such a state that our 4,000 followers were moved to the central block of terracing as the usual corner away area was disintegrating. Typical of the condition of so many grounds at the time. The Goldstone Ground is now a shopping centre, Palace fan Phil Nunn took his young son there and explained the rivalry which ended at the boy being encouraged to spit where the centre circle was.

Our Brighton rivalry is a weird one. I was travelling in Singapore and was sat on my own in a bar in a Palace top when I heard in a cheerful tone "All this way, and there some Palace tosser in the bar." I turned round and there were a couple of Brighton fans I didn't know who ended up buying me a few beers.

Still feeling deflated after losing one of our biggest matches of the season Dave Lewis and I got aboard coach 3 for the Friday night trip to Oldham. We left at 12.30 and got there very early, so much so that we had to have an extra stop otherwise the coach company would have been fined. The players had a rubbish journey back, the coach having a tyre blow out meaning they didn't get back to 5am. On a blustery evening we won 3-2, which on the dreaded plastic pitch was a good way to finish 1988. Phil Barber, Mark Bright and Geoff Thomas topped the appearance list for the calendar year with Ian Wright with 20 top of the goal scorers list.

We got near bye on 2nd January against Walsall, one of the worst teams I've seen at Palace. They couldn't cope with Bright, who got a hat-trick in his 100th game, or Wright who got the other. They were comical at times with most the crowd laughing and cheering when they strung three passes together which wasn't often.

We headed to Stoke for a cracking F.A Cup tie. A 1-0 defeat doesn't sound like a great game, but it was end to end and made our four-hour coach trip worth it. We may be six points from the play-offs but Robbie's cliché of "at least we can concentrate on the league" had a ring of truth about it.

We recruited Eddie McGoldrick during the week, a winger from Northampton for £200,000. With Salako and Dyer around as well clearly Coppell was trying to maximise the chances Wright and Bright would get. We still have little quality cover if either of those two are injured and Coppell dashed my hopes of getting a third striker as he declared that spending was over for this season. The following week Gareth Southgate signed his first professional contract. He was, like me, a former Hazelwick School pupil. There was worrying news when Mark Bright didn't seem keen on a new contract unless we got promoted.

After a Simod Cup win over Luton, we travelled to Chelsea but just didn't perform and lost to a Tony Dorigo free kick after Graham Roberts had faked to shoot to break up our wall. The crumbling open terrace was miles away from the pitch and even with 24,184 in the ground there was precious little atmosphere on a cold afternoon, made longer as we got in the ground just after 2pm rather than stop at a warm pub. A decision I didn't approve of. Few in the Palace end enjoyed their day: there were no reductions to the £5 admission for kids, inflatables were deemed unacceptable, we were kept in for 45 minutes after the game, programmes sold out, and the police initially refused to open one of the other sections of terrace despite the two being used becoming very full. Some were saying an accident will occur one day with overcrowding and no common sense being used. Noades later described the policing as "deplorable". Maybe it was he who had his inflatable banana confiscated.

Luckily it didn't rain to at Chelsea, but it chucked it down against Swindon at Selhurst. The pitch was sodden, and it must have been close to being called off. They took a first half lead, and it was looking like a dire afternoon. But up stepped Bright to score twice in a minute to win the game and keep us in with a hope of the play-offs. This was becoming more important with talk of our key players leaving if we didn't go up.

I gave the Simod Cup 4th round tie at Middlesbrough a miss, but Paul went and saw a staggering finish. With the game at 1-1 Boro got what seemed like an 88th minute winner, leaving Paul with a long solo coach ride back. But….Barber equalised instantly, and Wright got an injury time winner to put us into the Semi Finals. It's only the Simod, but also just one game from Wembley. Instead of that I went with Andy to see West Ham draw at Swindon. Their fans were hammering David Kelly – thank god we signed Bright and not him!

A more important victory came the following week at Ipswich. Wright put us two up in 25 minutes and we held on despite John Wark, in his 73rd season in league football, pulling one back and Hopkins getting sent off towards the end. The clueless referee later cancelled the red card as he had mistaken Hopkins for Pemberton. We had now made it into the play-off spots, a good effort after such a poor start to the season.

There was news of a scoreboard coming to Selhurst "hopefully in time for the Brighton game" said Clubby "keep track of how many we stick past those bastards".

We needed a late goal to get a point at home to Blackburn. It was a poor game and Rovers looked way more solid than in the "Timmons" game in October. Former Eagle Tony Finnigan was rather unpleasant after the game: "except for Wright and Bright, Palace don't have anything. I was glad to get away as I was kept out of the side by two-bit players." Paul reminded us the season wasn't over "We could still meet Blackburn again in May. Two-bit players may have the last laugh".

We drew a friendly at Southend, whilst I saw Andy's West Ham beat Charlton 1-0 at Selhurst in the F.A.Cup. "This is THE cup mate, not that Simod thing you are getting excited about." said Andy. Our Simod run did end that week at Forest, but we did equalise Neil Webb's early goal before David Burke was sent off and the impressive Stuart Pearce and another from Webb gave them a 3-1 victory. Some of Forest's passing was not something you see too much of in Division Two. Thanks to Suckling we stayed in the game throughout.

Yet another wet day saw a routine 2-0 win over Bradford, with Bright getting both. He added to his popularity shortly afterwards by signing a new contract which was great news. The match did see Geoff Thomas get injured, a big blow as he is likely to miss the rest of the season. Meanwhile Ron Noades was embroiled in a battle with the BBC. A play had been produced which showed hooliganism being portrayed at Selhurst and Noades felt this could harm the club's reputation; "our solicitors will review it with care" he warned "it seems they have incorporated Crystal Palace into it and have misrepresented the situation here."

One sad departure. Coppell's popular assistant Ian Evans left to join Swansea as manager. I hoped we may appoint Jim Cannon to replace him, but he opted for Stan Ternent previously manager at Blackpool.

Meanwhile our five a side team was going strong, and the next competition received some publicity in Crawley News as Palace sent Wright, Bright and Suckling down to Crawley as part of the Virgin sponsorship deal which will launch this summer's tournament. "Those three are rubbish" said West Ham Andy: "If we can beat Caledonian Old Boys we'd thrash those second division players."

We then dominated the game at Oxford, they didn't have a shot but won 1-0. Their miskicked winner coming direct from a corner. We slipped out of the play-off places and looked doomed to another year in division two when we lost 3-2 to Bournemouth. A sloppy display including a missed penalty from Wright and an ineffective midfield with Pardew suffering some fearful stick, sometimes with justification. How we missed Gray and Thomas in there. We were midtable now "It'll be an easy six points for West Ham next year" said Andy with his boys now marooned at the bottom of the first division. The way we played today I couldn't disagree. A feeling not helped by a good performance but only a draw at Barnsley, I was upset we didn't get a late penalty for a foul on Barber. The highlight at Oakwell was the Tommy Tyke article in the programme which was written in "Northern" with text such as "Owd 'of-stuff 'ad bin through a bit of a lean spell" kindly translated into English by Rob. After the game Salako went on to the transfer list, unhappy at not getting a game. Many thought he should start for Barber.

Our home game with Stoke was waterlogged off. Trev, Clubby and I pretended we missed the announcement and met at Selhurst anyway for too many beers in Crystals. The pitch recovered enough for Mark Bright to follow my advice and "whack the bloody thing" when we got a second half penalty to win 1-0 against Sunderland. Wright was going to take it but admitted he "bottled it".

West Ham Andy came to Watford with me "to see what we'll be up against next season" He wasn't too impressed by the game, but Barber's goal gave us the points. There was some bizarre half time entertainment with a pack of dogs hunting down a fictitious criminal and hauling him to the ground "We should do that with Brighton fans found in Croydon," said Trev.

Ron Noades made his views known on a few issues, particularly his disappointment that crowds were not reaching 10,000 and describing some performances as "rubbish" and players "not looking like they want promotion".

If there is a game to get to get the crowd going it's Brighton at home on a warm sunny day and this season's clash came with them fighting relegation. Even more incentive for us to win then! It was a crazy game "We'll get a penalty" Clubby said "Our mate Moreton is the referee. Get in!" We didn't get one, we didn't get two or even three – he gave us four, plus sent off Albion's Trusson in the first half! Wright put us ahead on 29 minutes with a stunning 35-yard volley from the left, then Bright buried a penalty and we were two up. McGoldrick earned us another penalty but that was saved, two minutes later Bright was fouled and another penalty awarded – which Wright smacked against the post. We were two up at half time but a third would have finished the game which was worryingly brought to life when a foul on Nelson gave Curbishley the chance to make it 2-1 from the spot. This made the game so much tenser than it should have been. We got our fourth penalty for handball, but this time Pemberton smacked it nearer to a beach hut in Sri Lanka than the net. We held on for a 2-1 win thanks to a fabulous last ditch scrambled save from Suckling when Curbishley should have equalised.

Ian Wright eased fears on his future "I've just committed myself to a long-term contract." The good mood came crashing down to earth with yet another awful display at Shrewsbury, losing 2-1. Trev and Vince had a heated row in the car on the way back on whether we would finish 9th or 10th and feeling equally disillusioned I abandoned plans to go to Leeds the following week. I played in a Moonraker pool match and heard the result on Palace Clubcall, on the third time of calling. I had got too nervous to hear the result the first two times. We had won 2-1.

Dave Madden was starting to find form in midfield and was excellent in a 2-0 win over Oldham, it was getting a little tense though until Bright's superb header added to Barber's opener. We were now up to 5th and well inside the play off places. "Things are starting to fall into place," said Coppell. If we made the play-offs I feared how I would cope with the tension, I had struggled to phone clubcall for a league result two days ago.

Paul and Jay joined me for a trip to Hull on the following Tuesday night. It took about five hours thanks to some diversions on the M18 and at one stage we were hopelessly lost in North Cave. The away end was two blocks of seats in a gale force wind, parallel to the penalty area. We saw a good performance with Pardew, now playing far better, and Madden controlling midfield and once Wright scored in first half injury time three more points were ours. The journey back seemed very long. Jay and Paul kipped off in the car as I motored down the M1. When I started to get tired, I pulled into a service station. They slept. I pulled out 20 minutes later. They slept. I did pull over for five minutes on the M25 to wake myself up a bit. They slept. I then dropped them off in Oxted "That was a quick journey back" grinned Paul. It was the last time I would ever drive to an evening away game, it's just too exhausting.

The following Saturday we played Portsmouth at home. We played well in the first half but it was 0-0. The FA Cup semi-finals were on and we heard Everton were leading Norwich but Liverpool's game with Forest had been delayed for reasons not given. We got the goals we richly deserved to win our game 2-0. When I got home Mum asked if I had heard the news and I was shocked to see what had taken place at the Hillsborough Semi Final where 96 people had died. The disaster arose as two central terrace pens became overcrowded when exit gates were opened to allow fans outside the ground in. They were not directed to the less packed wider areas and supporters at the front of the central section could not get over the six-foot fences and were crushed. It was nightmarish. It could have happened to any supporters around this time so could have been any of us in the makeshift mortuary at the back of the ground. It was an indication of how dangerous dilapidated grounds and high fences were. Fences were largely removed across the country, and the Taylor report would eventually lead to all seater grounds.

There was a minute's silence for Hillsborough at Plymouth. Clubby and I went for the £5.50 seats and watched us produce a very solid performance winning with a Bright goal in each half. The only blip was Pemberton's sending off. These three consecutive away wins have got us up to 4th, the play-offs look a near certainty now.

I had another trip to Swindon in the week. In a shambles of planning they had made it all ticket for Palace fans despite there being no home game between that announcement and the game, which they have had since August to re-arrange. We lost to a well taken first half goal. We made up for it with a 1-0 win over WBA which took us 8 points clear of the team outside the play offs, and a few cheeky eyes were seeing if we could catch Manchester City in the second automatic promotion spot. They were six points ahead of us, but we had a game in hand. Who do we play next…that'll be Manchester City!

It felt like a proper big game as Clubby and I got the 8.30am coach. A large Palace contingent helped boost the crowd to

33,360 and we all knew a win here and we could go up without the play offs. That hope was reduced when Gleghorn slid in to convert an 8th minute low cross. The same player ended up in goal as their keeper Dibble went off injured. It still looked like it was a lost cause until Wright popped up with a late equaliser to give us a good result, if not the dream one.

Clubby drove to Leicester where we thought we had won it with two Madden penalties, but Gary McAllister got a late equaliser. The point guaranteed our play-off position, and an amazing comeback from Bournemouth from three down to 3-3 at Maine Road meant in theory we could still go up automatically. On the way out of Leicester I said to Paul that this could be our last away game in Division Two for a while. Those slim hopes were maintained with Madden scoring the decisive penalty against Stoke. Rudi Hedman made his first start at right back looking none too solid.

To get promotion automatically on the final day we had to win, then hope Manchester City lost at Bradford and make up six goals in the process. Was it possible? Well just, as we were playing Birmingham at home who were already relegated.

Birmingham brought around 5,000 fans with them, many in fancy dress to have a relegation party. When Wright put us ahead there was chaos, thousands of them ran on to the pitch and started attacking people in the Arthur Wait Enclosure near the Holmesdale. I was towards the middle at the back of the enclosure so relatively safe, but it was clearly out of control and as there was a gap between the terrace and the wall, I saw no reason why they couldn't come along there and attack us where we stood. I eventually hid in the toilets upstairs near the Sainsbury's! Dead brave me! Eventually three police horses charged across the pitch and they shepherded the brummies back into the away end. The papers described them as "Sick evil scum" and the whole incident as "An orgy of violence "and "Brawl at the Palace".

Back on the pitch we slaughtered them to go four up by half time. Now, if City lost we only needed one more goal and we were up. We couldn't, could we? Yes, we dam well could! City were losing at half time!! Oh, my god!!! If they did not equalise and we scored one more we would be in the first division. It all went a bit flat though, when news of a City equaliser came through….and Birmingham even pulled one back so the play offs it was. Mind you it was still bloody exciting to be in them. Andy came over for a beer, his West Ham were relegated and he said he looked forward to playing us next season. But would they? Would we be in a higher league than them? Our deliberations on that resulted in a hangover the next morning.

*

We now entered the most important matches we had played for ten years.

Get through two two-legged ties and we would play in the first division next season. Nerves were building, not least as we had proved ourselves the third best team in the league already having finishing three points ahead of fourth placed Watford. We were to play Swindon in the two-legged semi-final.

The day before the semi-final first leg I got a ticket through Andy's uncle for the F.A Cup final. I had always said I would only go to Wembley should Palace get to a final, but as that seemed impossible, I said yes please. It was a great day even if it did feel like gate crashing a scouse party as Liverpool beat Everton, fittingly in view of Hillsborough. I insisted on not too many beers that evening as I had to get to Swindon the next day. That didn't really work out.

Palace had an allocation of over 5,000 tickets for Swindon available to members who could buy two each meaning the away terrace was full on a warm day. The tension was palpable in the ground. We all knew very well that if we didn't get through these play offs there was a massive risk we would lose our star strikers and may be destined for more years in division two.

We struggled in a feisty first half. Rudi Hedman looked nervous and clumsy at the back. Duncan Shearer thankfully missed a couple of chances. We hadn't got going, and it got worse after half time. A break down the right resulted in a dangerous low cross, Hopkins stuck out a leg and deflected the ball past Suckling for an own goal. They could have got another when Hopkins misdirected a header and Shearer ran through and smacked a shot against the bar, then Calderwood hit the bar too as we clung on to just the 1-0 deficit. The final whistle blew and we were mightily relived. We would play better in the second leg surely and were only one behind.

The atmosphere for the second leg at Selhurst was fantastic. You could feel it fizzing around the ground on a breathless sultry night, but behind that was a bundle of nerves as the teams emerged. It was loud, very loud.

We were brilliant in the first half, simple as that. We looked inspired, not daunted, by the atmosphere and threw everything at Swindon and after 9 minutes Bright scored to level the tie after a goalmouth scramble. Shearer did have a great chance to equalise, but thankfully didn't have the quality of our forwards. Minutes later Bright flicked on a free kick and Wright blasted it home and we led in the tie. One goal for Swindon though would put them through on away goals. The nerves were way too much for me to join the "going up" chants ringing around the ground particularly as Swindon threw everything at us towards the end. It needed Hopkins to throw himself in the way of a close range shot to prevent a late disaster. I kept my eyes on the ref and as he started to run towards the tunnel, I realised he was doing this as he was about to blew up and wanted to avoid the pitch invasion. It was emotional when he did. We would have one two-legged tie to decide if us or Blackburn Rovers would play in the first division next season. The crowd ran on the pitch to celebrate. Too soon for that I thought.

Before the final I had a trip to Anfield with Andy. West Ham needed a win to have any hope of staying up. They unsurprisingly got hammered 5-1. Andy drove to that, and we didn't stay over. We should have. He was clearly getting a little sleepy on the way home and with eyes closing he was heading towards a big lorry at on the M6. He then agreed with my stay over policy for future northern night games.

All this was byplay compared to our play-off final. Clubby, Rob, Trev and I started our near six-hour trip to Ewood with a pocket TV and a sports quiz book. We arrived early so the police escorted us to a pub that no Rovers fans were allowed in, so it felt like a Norwood boozer. A few optimistic chants started up as the rain came down outside and beers went down inside.

This game of monumental importance did not start well. After twenty minutes Garner's flick on was finished off by Howard Gayle who then added a second shortly afterwards with a shot from the edge of the box. The mood was gloomy at half time, as they looked worryingly comfortable. I was concerned they would get more in the second half and make the second leg irrelevant, which would be so sad as all 30,000 tickets had been sold. We did pick up a little but rarely looked like scoring until we got an 86th minute free kick on the halfway line. Bright got a header in ahead of keeper Gennoe and then McGoldrick bundled it over the line in front of delirious Palace fans who went berserk behind the goal. My heart rate was through the roof as I leapt around madly which was caught on the highlights. Wow, just one down now for the second leg – get in there! Just as we calmed down and looked up again there was a hammer blow. A header across the box was met by Garner to score for Rovers from close range. The whistle blew and we had lost 3-1. Too much to pull back surely. Our journey back was far quieter, and our thoughts moved to the upcoming five a side league as the first division now seemed as far away as ever. I was so disappointed, that third goal was a killer. When we arrived back at Selhurst around 2.15am Clubby's car wouldn't start. Luckily, my jump leads came to the rescue. We left that night talking about the joys of Oldham again next season "At least Shrewsbury went down," said Rob.

We had to beat Blackburn 2-0 to go up. 3-1 after extra time would result in penalties. They were a very solid team with Colin Hendry at the back and the prolific Garner up front. It didn't seem likely in all honesty. It was played on 4th June. It would be 31 years until we played a competitive game in June again and the circumstances would be very different then!

The atmosphere was of hope, rather than expectation as it had been against Swindon. It was a lively start, both teams looking dangerous. On 16 minutes a shrewd Barber pass found Pardew and with outside of the boot ("that's the part I like" commentated Brian Moore) he crossed, and Wright bundled the ball over the line. Cue pandemonium. We were back in it at 3-2 down on aggregate. The rest of the half passed by in increasing tension, not least during an amazing scramble in the Blackburn box. Our defence just couldn't make a mistake, but could we trust it? At least we had O'Reilly back in there for Hedman. Two minutes into the second half and with everyone around me almost too scared to watch, McGoldrick went down on the edge of the box. Referee Courtney pointed instantly and fantastically for a penalty. I was stood next to Andy at the top of the Enclosure and just said "I just can't look." It would be Madden to take it. The world stopped. Madden hit a perfect penalty into the corner. The outpouring of emotional celebration was deafening. I disappeared about halfway down the enclosure and finally clambered up to where Andy had remained. As things stood we were up. It was 3-3 but we had an away goal. If Rovers scored, they would be up. Only 73 minutes to survive as we would need to see out extra time too.

We made it to extra time. In the first period Wright had a golden chance running through on goal but Gennoe blocked it. With two minutes left and supporters already over the advertising boards close to the touch line we had a break down the right. I implored McGoldrick to get a free kick to waste time but he crossed and unmarked Wright headed in to put us 4-3 ahead. It was bedlam and a mini pitch invasion delayed the restart. We were so close, but if Rovers scored in the next few minutes we would have a penalty shoot-out. Suckling was forced into a cracking save tipping over Garner's shot before George Courtney looked at his watch and gloriously blew up.

We were promoted. It felt magical and emotional.

I went on the pitch with Andy and I stood in the centre circle in a daze of disbelief. He smiled and shook my hand and said, "wish we had stayed up to play you." I smiled "Hey mate, you can play us in a friendly, it'll be exciting for you to see a big first division team." He rolled his eyes.

All those trips up north, crushing defeats, managerial sackings, and desolation when it seemed that promotion would never come all seemed so worth it now. With the Yazz song "the only way is up" blasting out I looked over my shoulder on the way out from the top of the Holmesdale and saw so many smiling faces. I thought what would next year bring? Would we cope with the first division? Now was not the time to worry about that though, time for a drink!

As nobody expected it to happen, I had no idea where other friends were so Andy and I headed to Crawley and I drunk plenty of lager in the White Knight and thought who we could add to our squad to give us a chance of staying up.

From the depths of despair, we had done it and it felt bloody marvellous.

Glad All Over? You better believe it.

Chapter 9: Season 1989/90 – Hard Lessons Learned

We had endured some dark times over the last decade, but this summer was so very different. We were preparing for the top division and it was bloody exciting.

We were promoted largely because the Wright and Bright partnership up front was so strong, but as we were likely to be defending so much more it seemed vital to strengthen at the back. I liked the idea of Colin Hendry from Blackburn, we were reported to have bid £600,000 for him, and were linked with Andy Thorn at Newcastle, John Gittens from Swindon, Joe McLoughlin of Chelsea, and David Linighan from Ipswich. Obviously, there was the obligatory mention of Sunderland's Gary Bennett but none got close to arriving. Meanwhile we sold defender Gavin Nebbeling to Fulham for £80,000, and rumours continued that John Salako could leave as he had doubts that he would get much first team action.

I had decided in combination with Trevor Fitsall, now a regular in our five a side team, to arrange a sponsored walk to the first game of the season. We were joined by James, Vince Nemenyi, Paul Nowers and West Ham Andy. It was only to QPR, but we would raise some money for the St John's ambulance. I had the phone number of TACA, the shipping organisation where I worked, published in the Croydon Advertiser and that became our switchboard to discuss plans. Not a lot of work was done that summer, or in many summers, at TACA if truth be told. I even had some money coming in from a pen pal from Russia.

In the week leading up to the opener there was some staggering news. We re-signed Andy Gray from QPR for £500,000. At his best Gray was an awesome midfielder and with the old guard of Cannon, Droy and Wood no longer at the club, his main reasons for leaving had now disappeared. It will be great to see him back with Thomas. As part of that deal we also signed Mark Dennis for £50,000, a fearsome if injury prone left back with plenty of experience so that was a boost too. I still thought we were lacking in central defence and squad depth for the first division.

We also moved towards the nineties with news that a scoreboard would be erected at the Sainsbury's end of the ground. Some were not happy as they thought they were paying for that through ticket prices, for the first division these had jumped to between £6 and £17. The club did have some costs to cover in the next few years as we were moving towards all seater grounds following the Hillsborough disaster, and had announced the popular Arthur Wait enclosure would be seated from next season in accordance with the Taylor report.

Our season began with the now traditional trip to Sweden, one game saw the PA man struck by lightning. At home we won friendlies narrowly against Farnborough, then Clubby, Trev and I saw us win at Aldershot, but missed the return of Andy Gray in a 4-1 win at Swansea. The bigger friendly for me was Alan Devonshire's testimonial as we were playing Andy's West Ham. The Hammers won 3-1 but we had a good few beers in the Boleyn, but the toilets weren't the best. Someone hadn't quite managed to work out that once in a cubicle you were supposed to make deposits into the toilet bowl and not on the floor. Lovely. So second division I told Andy.

The fantastic Eagle Eye fanzine was out for the opening game and produced a list of predicted results for the season. This showed Palace winning every league match starting with a 6-1 away win at QPR on the opening day, and two 9-0 victories, clearly that's impossible as that score line never happens in top-flight football.

Our 13 mile walk to QPR, which raised £500, started at 7.30 and despite the odd stop for drinks we easily made kick-off.

The team were greeted by about 7,000 Palace fans and a crazy number of red and blue balloons. The atmosphere in the August sunshine was fantastic. We played well and showed that we could be competitive in this league but lost to two second half goals.

Three days later Selhurst was busy for the visit of Manchester United, our first home game back in division one. In the programme Coppell said how thrilled he was to be writing to us as a first division manager. It summed up how us fans felt. With expensive new signing Neil Webb joining England captain Bryan Robson in United's midfield it was always going to be tough. We put in a tremendous effort and deserved a last-ditch equaliser from Wright to level Robson's opener to get us our first top-flight point for over eight years. Ron Noades used the programme to have a big dig at the new TV deal giving advantages to the bigger clubs. "It stinks" he said.

When the fixtures came out an away game, followed by United, was going to be tough and I was hoping we would get the one point we did. A sign of whether we could stay in the league came when we played perennial strugglers Coventry. The weather was horrible, and our mood was no brighter as we lost to a free kick from man mountain Brian Kilcline. The rest of the game consisted of various blatant time-wasting tactics from a team who knew we were a club they would be fighting with to stay up and were determined to do whatever it took to get the points in front of a very disappointing 11,000 crowd. Andy Gray indicated he thought some of our players were not good enough for the first division.

Instead of going to Derry to watch Palace win a friendly I went with Andy to see his Hammers draw 1-1 at Hull. As we were coming out of the stand, we heard chants of "Hull, 'ull, 'ull" behind of us and we were set upon by some big northern fellas. Andy caught a punch that just ruffled his precious hair, I found a policeman to stand next to. It was all over in seconds but obviously we needed a few beers to get over it.

Palace desperately needed a result against Wimbledon, and got one, a 2-0 win. Their defence was terrible which was odd as they had Young, Scales and Curle in their line-up.

That gave us a boost before the trip to Anfield. Manager Coppell was aware it was a hell of a test, "my players are a little frightened" he admitted. They have more quality and matchwinners than any other side." It's only 11 v 11 I said. Andy said it should be OK, with a sense of irony. I was also worried by speculation linking Ian Wright with a £2m move to Anfield to replace John Aldridge who was about to leave for Spain.

On the coach there was a lot of black humour. Everyone knew that anything other than a thrashing would be a moral victory, Liverpool had been the best team in football for 15 years and as Jay said, "anything in single figures will be a result for us".

It was great just walking into Anfield. It has remained my favourite away ground full of atmosphere, history and with stands very close to the pitch. Liverpool players sauntered out for a warm-up with Martika's "Toy Soldiers" playing on the PA, followed by ours looking like kids who were somewhere they shouldn't be. From the first whistle Liverpool were magnificent. Silky movement, pinpoint crisp passing and brimming full of confidence supported by a crowd so used to victory it was routine. They were just an unstoppable machine. It was a wonder it took Steve Nicol seven minutes to lob the first, two more followed by half time. It was no surprise to be getting battered and we hoped they would ease off a bit in the second half. They didn't. Liverpool just got better and scored six more at the kop end. Each time a kid on our right held up fingers to tell us the score, at one point he lost count and had to ask his Dad how many it was now. To compound our misery we had a penalty, but Thomas whacked it halfway up the stand. Our section of the ground stayed in great spirits throughout and got quite a bit of praise still cheering away as goals seven to nine went in. We got back on the coach "Well, we did keep it to single figures, so not bad," said Jay. In a way "not bad" was true, we did play some decent stuff at times but just couldn't stop them when we didn't have the ball. With the ground and team so impressive the news that some Palace fans had suffered attacks from Liverpool's tainted the evening.

We were all over the radio one breakfast show the next morning with Simon Mayo dishing out plenty of jokes, and Capital Radio DJ's wearing black armbands. Andy joined in at work, I had copies of the Sun's "9-0" headline everywhere from desk drawers, to my car dashboard, to my tea mug. These included quotes from captain Thomas. "we were drowning in a sea of red", "I felt helpless" and "it was the most vicious demolition". Our keeper Perry Suckling, unfairly, became a target for the papers with even cartoonist Mahood joining in. Suckling vowed to "forget it". Good luck I thought.

We did regain pride quickly, a creditable 1-1 draw at Southampton which after the hoo hah of the Liverpool game was a good achievement.

We played very well the following week Richard Shaw making his league debut as we beat Forest 1-0 thanks to a late but richly deserved Wright goal. We attacked their left side relentlessly in the first half taking advantage of the formidable Stuart Pearce's absence. My memory of the game was trying to find a quiet spot to stand in as I had a ferocious headache. I had been out on the Friday night with Andy. I was sure that had nothing to do with it.

The following Saturday I thought we really arrived as a first division club, we played to our full potential to beat an experienced Everton team 2-1. We were full of pace and energy in the first half as Wright and Pardew put us two up. There was renewed confidence in our defence that withstood a barrage of pressure once Newell pulled one back. We were up to 9th now, not the laughingstock of a few weeks ago. Coppell knew we could get better pointing out that Andy Gray was the only player we had with first division experience.

We got past Leicester on away goals in the League cup. I only listened on the radio as I had a horrific bout of flu and stayed awake just long enough to hear the final whistle had blown.

The club were considering moving from Selhurst to the National Sports Centre up the road. It would become a 60,000 capacity "super stadium" which was a requirement if we wanted to become part of a European Super League that was being mooted. Noades was complaining that local residents caused issues if we tried to develop Selhurst and saw this as a great opportunity. "Plenty of space, travel access and will not infringe the lives of local residents". 60,000? Really, I thought? We only got 11,000 the other week! Noades was also concerned about the government's ID scheme "you could be forgiven for thinking that they may be looking at games hoping there is crowd trouble" as he implored fans to be on their best behaviour.

John Salako had rejoined us after being with Swansea on loan. This had gone well and there was an expectation that he would be competing to win back his spot in the Palace team. It was good to have another squad member with O'Reilly and Dennis injured.

A crew of Andy, Rob, James, Trev, and I booked an overnighter for the trip to Derby staying at the splendid Grosvenor Hotel for a paltry £12 each. During our night out we had the dubious pleasure of meeting the apparent "Leader of the Derby boys." He seemed perplexed at our complete disinterest in any kind of trouble, so we carried on drinking and playing pool. He did tell us to avoid the Blue Peter pub which we duly did, good job to a there was a "hell of a punch up there" according to our waiter at brekkie. The game was dire, we got stuffed 3-1 with Saunders a constant threat, but it was a fun trip.

The following week saw a Selhurst classic. Millwall were also going well and were a tough team. We started in true Palace comedy style, five minutes in and Hopkins lobbed it over Suckling for a spectacular own goal from thirty yards. Then we played very well, full of pace with the old firm of Wright and Bright superb and we deserved our 3-1 half time lead. Millwall got going after that and a fine Cascarino header made it 3-2 and we started to wilt under their considerable pressure, and it was no surprise when Anthrobus levelled the game. They had all the momentum and looked sure to get an inevitable winner. A rare second half break though saw the ball fall to Bright who slammed in a great shot from the edge of the box with three minutes left to give us the points. A breathless, thrilling game won 4-3 that summed up our strengths and defensive weaknesses perfectly.

Meanwhile we lost Glenn Pennyfather to Ipswich for £80,000 and were apparently interested in bringing in Ray Wilkins from Rangers. We certainly needed more in midfield, Gray and Thomas were top class but below that our quality fell off a cliff. After all, nobody thought Pardew was likely to do anything significant.

We drew Nottingham Forest in the League cup. It was 0-0 despite us dominating the game. A replay would be needed. This would become a familiar tale.

Next was a trip to Aston Villa. Well, a trip towards Aston Villa would be more accurate. Clubby and I left Tadworth at 10.15, and we had ample time to stop for coffee at Toddington services. A few yards after pulling out the car starting chugging away and ground to a halt as we pulled onto the hard shoulder. I had AA membership, so they came and fixed the car much to our relief in good time, having made it clear to the mechanic what time the game kicked off, and we carried on heading to Villa. Five minutes later we had the same problem and the AA towed us to Newport Pagnell services. By the time we left it was already close to kick-off, so we decided to head to a game at Northampton Town instead, only for the car to conk out for a third time. This time Clubby phoned his

Dad who volunteered to come and tow us home. Whilst waiting three hours for him to leave Tadworth we found a hotel for lunch and listened to radio commentary from Villa. Our day was complete when a last-minute goal from David Platt handed us a defeat to go with our broken-down car. Clubby's Dad won the man of the match award as we got back at 11pm.

In the week we got hammered 5-0 at Forest in the replay. They were four up by half time and we were outclassed. We got no better the following week when Rob and I got the £12 coach to Manchester City with two experts-on-anything types in front of us both ways. We got beat 3-0 with Suckling looking like his confidence was shot, but he wasn't being given much chance with the way we were defending. At least the day finished with a few pints and games of pool in Thornton Heath. The spirit in the team seemed to be missing for spells in the Luton home game. Suckling had been replaced by Brian Parkin in a 1-1 draw and we had started to slip down the table. The mood certainly seemed suspect, with rumours of a bust up between assistant manager Alan Smith and Dave Madden. Maybe the arrival of Ian Branfoot as a coach would help. We were, yet again, linked with defender Gary Bennett in view of our dodgy defending.

Realising the issues in goal the club took the plunge and became the first to spend £1m on a goalkeeper, not a well-known one but Nigel Martyn from Bristol Rovers. Really? Is he that good? How about the defence, surely that's the main issue? Jim Cannon weighed in saying Martyn had walked into a "keepers' nightmare" and saw the defence as the main issue and many fans agreed. Suckling vowed to fight for his place, it didn't seem likely that he'd succeed.

Martyn made his debut at home to Tottenham with Gascoigne in midfield at a packed Selhurst which produced record receipts of £156,000. None of this helped our shaky defence though. Bright put us ahead but two minutes later we were behind with Howells scoring plus a Lineker penalty. Bright levelled but it was no surprise when Spurs got a winner, albeit through a deflection. It was a cracking game though and the atmosphere was the total opposite of what we were enduring on dour days five years earlier.

On a bitterly cold day we travelled to struggling Sheffield Wednesday, scene of the nightmarish Hillsborough disaster just seven months earlier. It was sobering to see the area below us with twisted crash barriers giving a silent reminder of the horrors that day. We should have coasted to victory once Gray and Hopkins had put us two up but with referee Scott seemingly only able to point in the home teams favour we ended up drawing 2-2 thanks to a last-minute penalty given away by the clearly gutted McGoldrick. It was harsh on Martyn, who made several excellent saves.

The ZDS Cup, the third cup introduced during English clubs' European ban, had us drawn at home to Luton. On paper it was likely to be a forgettable game. However, my interest was heightened once Kelvin Morton was named as the ref, he who had given us four penalties against rivals Brighton last season. This time he sent off two of their players plus a coach (too much merriment as it was former seagull Danny Wilson) as we romped home 4-1 winners. Kelvin even grinned at the crowd as the "there is only one Kelvin Morton" chant went up.

Not much joy on the Saturday though, a demoralising 3-0 home defeat to QPR on a dull afternoon with veterans Peter Reid and Ray Wilkins showing way too much streetwiseness for us. The atmosphere was a little strange as one of the Holmesdale terrace compounds were closed as work was taking place to increase its capacity. It was a sobering defeat that left us in the relegation zone.

We then made an important signing, experienced ex Wimbledon defender Andy Thorn for £650,000 from Newcastle. We also picked up Darren Carr a winger for £60,000 from Burton.

We stayed over for Manchester United away with Trev, Rob, Paul, Jay, Robbie, Andy, and I all getting the benefit of Rob taking advantage of a printing error to get a top-notch hotel for £20 each. At least we thought we'd have somewhere comfortable to enjoy after surely another fruitless trip up north. United started well and Beardsmore put them ahead. Martyn made a couple of magnificent saves in front of the Stretford end to keep us in the game. However, we improved. Bright levelled just before half time and then bundled home another after the break. The locals were furious. Alex Ferguson was getting fearful stick with the vast majority of the crowd screaming for his dismissal. We found the excellent Bollington pub and celebrated the glory of "Manchester United 1 goal, Crystal Palace 2 lovely goals". We briefly gate crashed a wedding reception before I collapsed in my hotel room in time for the third-round cup draw. We had Portsmouth at home. The following day the local headline "Fergie's head on the block" summed up how close he was to the sack.

We won the away home game "at" ground sharers (and rivals in their eyes) Charlton. The whole affair even had a lengthy feature on the "Saint and Greavsie" show and showed our away supporters club planning a coach tour around London to make it feel like an away game. You wondered why that was necessary, but the media lapped it up. The two wins, with Martyn and now Thorn settled in the team, had seen us rise to 12th. Three days later we knocked Charlton out of the ZDS in sheeting rain to upset them even more. Our group missed the game as we were busy finishing third in the far more important Crawley five a side league.

We had our traditional family Boxing Day do in Hastings, but I was determined to make Palace v Chelsea as it was a 12.30 kick off. I got to the Purley Way junction when my car just stopped and started backfiring, I couldn't start it and traffic was building up behind me and there was much tooting. I felt a bit panicky. Eventually I got out the car and a fella in the van behind kindly helped me push it over a very busy roundabout and into the Magnet car park. Time was ticking towards kick off, so I left the car and ran to the ground. I stopped to call the AA and gave my cars location but explained I wouldn't be with it as I'd be at Selhurst Park. "Hope you win" the operator said, "I don't like Chelsea." I got in the ground to see Dixon score early and late, but a 2-2 draw was OK. I then ran back to the Purley Way and found the AA had sorted my car out.

We finished the decade, as we started it, at home to Norwich. We won this time thanks to Wright's header which capped an excellent team performance. I was more than happy with 14th. Suckling, with no chance of getting back in the team, went on loan to West Ham.

Arsenal away, on the first day of the nineties, was a 4-1 thrashing. It could have been 10-1 they were that good. We went back and had a few pints in the Duke of York in Victoria. When we picked the papers up it was reported that Palace were considering re-signing Clive Allen, we were all sceptical about that.

We were given 66-1 odds to win the FA Cup, but those reduced a little when Andy Gray blasted home a dodgy late penalty to beat Portsmouth in a low-key game. We then lost at Coventry when our offside trap was breached by Speedie with an icy gale blowing towards us in the small low terrace.

Liverpool arrived at Selhurst and we obviously feared the worst. My mum joined us and got quite wound up by cheering Liverpool supporters when they scored, "I can understand why people punch them!" They were once again as smooth as silk but thankfully settled for just the 2-0 win this time. Noades wasn't happy with referee Bodenham "it's like officials expect Liverpool to win." The bigger problem was Ian Wright breaking his leg, so he'll be out for months. My Mum had seen Ian Evans have his leg broken by George Best in 1977 so most players will not be relish seeing her turn up too often. After the match Dave Madden, so influential last season, joined

Birmingham on loan following rumours of a falling out with management.

Off the field there was concern at many clubs of the cost of going all-seater following the reports into Hillsborough. For Palace it was quoted at a staggering £22m to preserve the current capacity. The Taylor report was also critical of the treatment of away supporters: "law-abiding fans are caught up in a police operation reminiscent of marching prisoners of war." Very true I thought, but it had taken disasters such as Hillsborough for the media not to jump on the football supporter bashing bandwagon.

We had a good fourth round cup draw and beat Huddersfield comfortably 4-0. Clubby and I even sneaked a drink into the game, such rebels, and discussed the slim chances of getting revenge for the League cup defeat at Forest as we booked our coach for the league game. We lost that 3-1.

With the clutches of relegation snapping at us we needed a win against Southampton. We got it too with a 3-1 victory. They didn't take their chances, we did. Salako, who had been subject of a Saints bid earlier in the season, got the first and was relishing his role back in the first team in Wright's absence.

Again, we got a good cup draw, this time Rochdale at home. Should be another walkover I thought. It certainly wasn't with their keeper Welch making a series of stunning saves and an unattractive replay loomed until Barber put us ahead. However, with the referee looking at his watch Rochdale had a rare attack and looked certain to equalise from close range, but Martyn produced a wonder save and we were into the quarter finals.

Having got past Swindon in the ZDS we then lost to Chelsea at home in the area final. With Wembley close it was a depressing evening, and we lost the second leg too. The arrival of Sheffield Wednesday gave us a chance to lift that gloom, but a very uninspiring afternoon left us with just a point which was better than it sounded after Bright scored but was sent off for a stamp on Madden.

We had a great win at Spurs, a looping Pardew header getting us the points. This gave us breathing space at the bottom in a game I had no optimism about. They had a stack of chances at the end, and many others joined me in barely watching numerous goalmouth scrambles. Luckily none of the chances fell to Lineker.

When we drew Cambridge in the FA Cup quarter final Andy told me "Your name is on the cup mate, another easy draw." There was no doubt I fancied us to beat them. We did have a group of players who were certainly not fancy Dans or afraid of such a tight tricky ground. The big talk pre-game was if Wright would play. He had made an amazingly quick return from the leg break which would be handy as Bright was unavailable. Nobody knew for certain, until he ran out for the warm-up. It was a difficult game, they had two massive lads up front in Dublin and Taylor and they were a right handful and Cambridge shaded the first half. The second period was nervy, but we won it when a shot from Thomas bobbled through the penalty area and over the line and my God we were in the Semi Finals of the Cup! The last time that happened my Dad had to make me a stool to stand on in 1976.

The following day was the semi-final draw. Just one match from a dream of seeing us in a cup final. We would draw one of Oldham, Manchester United who were full of big names but beatable, or the all-conquering mighty favourites Liverpool. Please, just don't give us Liverpool I prayed. We drew Liverpool. I was heartbroken. I slammed the lounge door in frustration. No chance of making Wembley now after all the drama at Villa Park.

Clubby and I brought tickets from a tout outside the ground at Everton, "They are in the away end lads." We promptly found out they weren't, but were good seats anyway, but watched us get hammered 4-0. The local papers were predicting Liverpool may even eclipse the nine they got against us in the upcoming semi-final in view of our shambolic defending. With Pemberton going off with a nasty injury, that took ten minutes to treat with a defibrillator, it was not the best of afternoons. Post-match beers and a curry made up for it.

Disaster struck in the Derby home game, a bitterly cold night that had two frustrations. Firstly, a late Mark Wright header meant we only drew, but more worryingly another broken leg for Ian Wright which could have a huge impact on our chances of staying up, and at least giving Liverpool a game in the semi. Rudi Hedman started at full back and was shocking, nowhere near first division standard.

We did bring in a forward to cover for Wright's injury, burly striker Garry Thompson for £200,000. He was superb on his debut, full of enthusiasm and got a vital early winner against Villa which got us up to 14th. With Richard Shaw marking their pacy winger Carr out of the game it was a very good performance. We backed this up with three more points, this time at Millwall to lift us nine points clear of the bottom three. Surely that will do it! The players may have thought the same, or had an eye on the semi-final, as we put in a lacklustre display at Norwich losing 2-0 on a cold night. The highlight was a good few beers in a local pub that looked more like Crystals bar at Selhurst with lots of familiar faces.

Next game, Liverpool at Villa Park, F.A.Cup Semi Final. The papers were full of it. "Sweet dreams are made of this, but not for you Palace" was a typical headline. Nobody disagreed. Nobody expected anything other than a thrashing. Andy was working out how long he could take the piss for. "Do you want me to keep score?" As it was the first semi-final to be live on the BBC, I feared national shame after the 9-0.

We all booked into the Penguin Hotel on the Saturday night and had a good evening out. A Liverpool fan came over with a tray of beers. "Here you go lads, it's all you'll be getting this weekend." We had a great buffet breakfast, which was much in need to sort a couple of hangovers. "Condemned man's last meal for you boys" grinned a fella in a Liverpool top.

The game started quietly, Liverpool generally on top as expected. With only fourteen minutes gone, Rush sprinted through our defence and slotted the ball efficiently past Martyn, and we were behind already. Liverpool barely celebrated, their goal being so inevitable to them. We hung on to half time so were technically still in the match. Pundits were giving us no chance but former boss, the flamboyant Malcolm Allison, did predict this was far from over.

With the second half ten seconds old Pemberton made a staggering run down the right and sent in a cross, shots were blocked, and it was chaos until Bright slammed it in. My God we are level! There was utter chaos around me with everyone leaping all over each other, a stark contrast to the reaction to their goal. On 69 minutes the unthinkable happened. Another scramble and this time O'Reilly slammed it in. My God we are winning!! How is this possible? Now I felt ill. Suddenly we had something to lose. As if that wasn't dramatic enough, I saw Jay Sisley who I went to so many second division away games with being taken out in a wheelchair. It turned out he was fine.

Our dreams had got within ten minutes of the final whistle when another Liverpool attack ended with a dodgy free kick which found its way to McMahon who slammed a shot into the top corner. Then seconds later Staunton went down oh so easily and referee Courtney gave them a penalty which Barnes put beyond Martyn's reach. 3-2 down. Oh well, magical whilst it lasted we thought. Then as the tension had left us it was back Andy Gray heading an equaliser 3-3. I can't cope with this I thought. As Rob had said the previous night "it's the hope that kills you." Then my dreams flashed in front of my eyes as in injury time as Thorn rose for a header. Is this the winner? I felt feint! The ball hit the bar and bounced away. So, so close. We would go to extra time. Whatever happened we had made a game of it. Even Andy would have to admit that.

The first half of extra time was relatively quiet. A replay was looking likely when we got a corner with eleven minutes of extra time left. It was headed on at the near post by Thorn and Pardew stormed in to give us a 4-3 lead. Everyone was exhausted by now, so the celebrations were now slightly muted as our end was shattered with the nervous tension. This is it I thought. We have 10 minutes to survive. I tried to pass the time with a walk to the back of the stand, where there was a guy being sick with tension "I just can't watch mate." I tried to light a cigarette and failed dismally as I didn't smoke. Anything to pass a few seconds. I looked up and saw Martyn save brilliantly from Barnes. They have the best team in Europe, surely we can't do this. I swear to this day the clock behind me on the Holte end was broken or operated by a scouser. It just did not move. It was on 119 minutes for about three weeks. When it ticked to 120 the Palace end made referee Courtney very aware. I couldn't not take my eyes off him, just blow the bloody thing I thought as they swept forward yet again. Eventually he got his whistle out, it went to his lips, and he blew up to end a breathless match. I was stunned, these things just didn't happen to us.

We would be in the FA Cup final and had won the greatest FA Cup semi-final ever seen. The emotion of all around us was incredible. If anyone in our end wasn't in tears they must be lying. Wright hobbled on with his crutches, and Coppell legged it off overcome with it all. It was without doubt the most stunning match I had seen or will surely ever see. I'd had a sneak preview of Wembley this season with Andy watching England beat Brazil and Czechoslovakia. I couldn't bring myself to imagine Palace walking out for a cup final. I certainly made it very clear to everyone at work who had laughed at our 9-0 loss back in September what had happened with my scarf raised proudly above my desk. Even Andy had to agree "Amazing mate." To this day I feel so emotional watching that game, particularly our first goal. John Sadler summed it up in the papers "Best telly since they landed on the moon" and Harry Harris "They stole the hearts of the nation".

It then dawned on me that I had to drive home. I was in no state to do that for a while, so I laid on a grass bank with a couple of coke's just trying to calm down a little. Eventually Clubby found me and we sat and in shattered silence for a while having no idea how that just happened, Rob finally broke the silence "I saw you trying to light up" and just laughed at me. He has never forgotten.

Our Belgian friend Carmen joined my Dad and I for the Palace home game against Arsenal with "Scousebusters" and "Super-Al" T-shirts on sale. A bumper 28,000 crowd gave the team a great reception and they were on such a high we played Arsenal off the park for the first ten minutes. A goal from Hayes against the run of play suddenly made this seem like an "after the Lord Mayor's show" affair. I was pleased Carmen saw us score though when a late Gray goal got us a point, but there was a worry over Andy Thorn who picked up an injury. I had to leave Carmen straight after the game for beers in Baker Street with Andy and Paul, a Man United fan, our opposition in the final.

We got well beat at Chelsea the following week and O'Reilly was sent off. We sat in the warm spring sunshine chilling out after the stress of the previous weekend on the unpopular away terrace.

If we beat Charlton we would be in the first division next season. Not only that but we could relax and enjoy the build up to the final. All was set fair on a sunny afternoon at Selhurst, and second half Thompson and Bright goals got us the valuable points, after Charlton had thankfully missed some sitters. Such a relief Palace didn't "do a Palace" and mess this one up. During the week there had been uproar that we only received 14,000 tickets for the cup final, but disappointing only 15,000 turned up against Charlton to give ammunition to those who defended the policy. Noades remained furious accusing the FA of lacking integrity. Some clubs, led by West Ham, agreed with him and let us have their ticket allocation. United had received 26,000.

The last few games didn't seem too important, it was all about the cup final build up. There were photos of Pardew, Gray, O'Reilly and Bright reproducing the Beatles Abbey Road picture, and a catchy cover of "Glad all over" as the club song with the splendid "Where Eagles fly" as the 'B' side.

One of our remaining games was at Luton where away fans were banned. So obviously I still went in my car with Paul, Rob and Clubby. We thought removing car stickers and scarves from view would make all the difference. We had borrowed West Ham Andy's membership card. He was able to get one thanks to a connection in Wycombe. We casually wandered around the ground trying subtly to get some idea how we used this card to get four tickets. We made no secret of who we were supporting once inside but had little to cheer as Dowie scored their late winner on the horrible plastic pitch.

Our last away game of the season was at Wimbledon. It was very physical and we nicked it with Bright's excellent header. We finished off with a light hearted game in the sun against Manchester City. We went two up on the crest of a pre cup final wave but faded. Quinn got a last-minute equaliser after Thompson had been sent off, not that anyone cared in a carnival atmosphere. Both sets of fans ended up on the pitch chatting and having a game of 100 a side football with their friendly supporters wishing us well against their rivals the following week.

The cup final build up carried on with pictures of Noades, his wife Novello and Richard Branson at Wembley plus daily feature length articles on our players who had come so far in recent years. The week leading up to the game seemed to go on for ever, but eventually the Friday night dawned. "Beer tonight?" asked Andy, for once I replied, "Can't mate, must feel well tomorrow."

It was a traditional cup final day. TV schedules starting at 9am and it was bright, warm, and sunny. The only difference was I was going to see Palace in it. Unbelievable! I left Three Bridges at 11.30 and as we pulled into East Croydon the joy and hope on people's faces was an inspiring sight. So many had a look that said this is some reward for those years of struggle, and even at this early hour it was emotional.

I met many of the usual faces Clubby, Paul, Rob, Robbie, Trev, and Jay in Victoria all grinning and we had a couple of drinks before getting on a very noisy tube with traditional Palace songs booming down the escalators and on to the trains with red and blue scarves and flags dominating every carriage. We changed at Baker Street for the quick service into Wembley Park. The walk from the station to the ground, a straight line looking right at the mighty stadium was magical. I had dreamt about something like this during the bitter winter in Canada or trudging back out of Selhurst losing in front of 4,000. Wow. I mean wow. We even saw the team coach drive by with everyone wishing the team luck from the bottom of their hearts.

I was sat with Clubby in the £35 seats close to the halfway line in block 122 and we saw Manchester radio beat Capital in a fun penalty shoot-out. A few of our team came out to warm up. "lovely Jubbly" said the guy behind me. We had "Abide with Me" echoing around the ground, a marching band, and you could see red and blue balloons at the ready in our end behind the goal. All was set. Brilliant. The teams came out and it was surreal, the noise was deafening, the balloons were staggering, pouring out of our end like bubbles out of a never-ending bottle of champagne. We were just so excited.

The game was initially quite dull. After 20 minutes we won a free-kick, and a scramble came off O'Reilly and the ball looped past Leighton and Palace were winning 1-0. I tried not to let my heart race, so early I thought. Sadly true. Robson's deflected shot made it 1-1 after 33 minutes so all level at half time. Too tense to talk at half time. A cruel deflection off Thorn fell to Hughes after 59 minutes and he swept it past Martyn and we were 2-1 down. Clubby gave me an "oh-well" look. Despite being passed fit Coppell had decided to leave Wright, back from injury, on the bench but he was desperate to get on and he replaced Barber on 71 minutes. This was our last throw of the dice. Seconds later Wright picked the ball up on the far side and ignored all round him and charged towards the penalty area. He made Pallister fall over, shot past Leighton and we were back level at 2-2. He celebrated wildly; our fans celebrated wildly. Emotions were uncontrollable for many.

Three minutes into extra time Salako sent over an inch perfect cross which caught Leighton out and there was Wright to volley us into a 3-2 lead. Pandemonium. Can we hold on for 27 minutes was all I was thinking. We had 15 minutes left at half time in extra time and then got halfway through the second period. At this point I started to think it would be our day, seven minutes left.

I gazed up to where in about 10 minutes Geoff Thomas could be going up to lift the F.A. Cup and the thought of that was just something out of a fantasy book. It was so so close. I wanted it so much not just for now but also for those trips to northern outposts in freezing weather, desperate calls home from Canada hoping for a draw at Grimsby, sleeper trains home from Sheffield, suffering two relegations in my first two years of supporting Palace, and for my group of friends and family to enjoy a day which was truly ours on the global stage.

As I gazed back down again Hughes shot past an advancing Martyn and the ball rolled over the line. 3-3. Both teams were shattered, and it would go to a replay.

Was I disappointed? You bet I was. But another trip to Wembley and a second game with more Palace supporters allowed sounded good, and our finances will get another boost. I met Andy for a drink that night. It had been quite a day and at the end of the evening he knew every detail about it and asked if I could get him a replay ticket.

The following morning I joined the ticket queue at Selhurst at 6.30am for Thursday's replay. It took hours to get to the front as the line went round two massive car parks and the nearby roads. They didn't start selling until 10.30! It sounds grim, but like similar queues for the semi and final we had plenty of giggles and most importantly made sure we got tickets. The increased allocation of 26,000 made it a lot less stressful than when we only had 14,000. Luckily the weather was good!

We changed kit to black and yellow for some reason, it is not well remembered. Largely because the replay didn't have any of the magic of the first game or the day itself. Our cause wasn't helped when their dodgy keeper Leighton was replaced with Les Sealey. Palace were criticised for an over physical approach and we surely should have started with Wright and not left him on the bench. We should have had a first half penalty for a foul on Thomas, but we did get to half time at 0-0. United scored on the hour, full back Lee Martin running through, and with a hint of handball, fired past Martyn. We rarely looked like equalising and the final whistle ended what had been an amazing season.

I didn't feel too amazing at that point. I walked straight out of the stand having no desire to see Robson lift the cup and sat on the concrete steps leading to the exit. A few Palace fans walked past me. "Don't worry mate, we'll be back soon." I felt so deflated.

Would we? It would take another 26 years.

Andy came along, lifted me up, and we went for a much-needed drink.

I went home and finished my season's stats. Player of the year was Andy Gray. He also had most appearances and was only behind Bright and Wright in the goal scorers list.

I just thought this time stats just don't tell the story of a very special season.

Chapter 10 – 1990/91: Potential reached.

Much of the country finally realised what a great game football was in 1990. I had loved it from going to my first Palace game as a six-year-old with my Dad, to the dark days of the early eighties, and even the heartbreak of our F.A.Cup final defeat. There is little in a typical week that can give the emotional roller coaster that being a passionate supporter can bring, both the highs and the lows. The World Cup "Italia 90" brought a monumental change of public perception. Instead of people calling for football to be banned, now a crying Geordie had the public caught up in footy fever.

After the cup final Palace had a tour to the Caribbean. It was a mystery that West Ham Andy and I didn't have a holiday to enjoy that. Mind you we did make windswept Blackpool, with Rob, Jay, Robbie, and Paul - same thing really! There we saw England take on the Germans in the epic World Cup semi-final. I was left nearly as gutted as I was after the cup final replay as we messed up the penalty shoot-out. The joy we took winding Jay up on a ride on the pleasure beach made up for the disappointment. We all realised a safety bar wasn't needed on one ride, but he didn't. "Got your bar down Jay?" His look of sheer panic as the ride started made me forget Pearce and Waddle's penalty misses.

Back home a few transfers that didn't happen started our summer, Salako to Metz for £1m and Andy Linighan from Norwich who we would go on to sign a few years later. We were also linked with star World Cup defender Gica Popescu, which sounded fantastic as did a reported offer of £2.5m for England's Mark Wright. A £1m move for Vinny Jones was also mooted.

We did pick up John Humphrey, a solid first division right back from Charlton for £450,000 which led to the popular John Pemberton joining Sheffield United for a bit less. Then midfielder Glyn Hodges arrived from Watford for £500,000, a couple of summers later we played five a side against him at Staplefield.

Our hopes of Popescu faded, seemingly issues with the Romanian Sports Minister, and instead we were underwhelmed with the signing of Eric Young from Wimbledon for £850,000. His Brighton past didn't help his reputation with the supporters.

We also lost Madden to Maidstone and Burke to Bolton, but most thought we had done good business. We were 100-1 to win the league, whilst Ladbrokes had us as joint favourites to go down as Andy pointed out with considerable relish during a lunch hour around Crawley. The local press thought it would still be a tough season, with anything around 14th come May considered a success.

I heard about our team bonding friendly victories in Sweden on clubcall sitting at TACA, still my happy shipping workplace. The friendlies in England were not too inspiring. A narrow win at Colchester and draws with Hull and Bristol City, then defeat to Fiorentina and a draw with Sampdoria meant we had some top-level opposition. A stark contrast to the dour football league trophy a few years ago!

Rob, Clubby and I joined about 2,000 Palace fans for the opener at Luton, which was strange as they still banned away fans. Eric Young was excellent on his debut and any doubts over his signing evaporated straight away as he put us ahead, but Dowie's equaliser meant we settled for a draw. We had a shocking view with six pillars in the way and then got stuck in a long traffic jam. I even had to call the AA when the car broke down on the way home. The joys of football travel were back.

The first home game against Chelsea was on lovely sultry night, with Timmy Mallet's dot bikini song banging out pre-game. It was classic blood and thunder stuff with Gray's early penalty putting us ahead, then a ruck between he and Wise saw both sent off as tackles flew in. Wright put us two up with a superb chip before a deflected goal gave Chelsea hope in a frantic finish. A breathless start for the new look Arthur Wait stand with seats replacing the popular terrace to comply with the post Hillsborough Taylor report.

With Bright missing for the first two games Garry Thompson was partnering Wright and he got the winner against Sheffield United in a very convincing display on a sun-drenched afternoon. The crowd of 17,000 gave the returning Pemberton a greater reception than Bassett, our former boss, who rejected us after three weeks in 1984. "Hey Andy, we are fourth" I said on Monday. "You won't finish there he said." True I reluctantly agreed.

Palace were getting good reports with Wright, who had just signed a new four-year deal, and Martyn both being tipped to make the next England squad. Our reputation grew when Vince's £50 car got us to Norwich to see us demolish them 3-0. The £50 "good little runner" started making a strange noise as we got closer to home, "best stop at that pub" said Clubby. I agreed. We were up to second, only once in our history had we been higher, on that golden afternoon in 1979 so pints were called for.

Andy and I went on holiday to Rhodes the following week for another cracking trip. On the Saturday, my attention on the sandy beach was on my massive radio as a win could put us top of the first division. Shaw put us ahead, but I then assumed my radio had malfunctioned as they seemed to say Martyn had made a mistake and Pearce had equalised. Martyn? Mistake? Peace then scored a worldie from a free-kick to give them the lead, but Thomas equalised with a brilliant header in the last minute. I left for the Faliraki bars to hear the KLF's "What time is Love" everywhere having to settle for remaining unbeaten in fourth. Oh well!

With Lineker and Gascoigne passing late fitness tests a trip to high flying Tottenham was always going to be tough, and when the crying Geordie and World Cup star Gazza curled in a free kick it looked like our unbeaten start would end. However, a late Thomas goal was very well celebrated in the packed away end. After the game I heard a group of Spurs fans saying how impressive we were, particularly Thomas. Maybe we could even finish top half!

In the good old days when teams played their first-choice teams in the League cup we destroyed Southend 8-0. We wanted nine at the end.

A group of us stayed over in Derby on the following Saturday, and even Andy agreed we looked so strong as we won 2-0 thanks to the old firm Wright and Bright. The only downside to our trip was the slack service in Pizza Hut, but Trev got us free drinks out of it. When I woke up in the morning, I wish he hadn't.

We didn't reproduce that form at home to Leeds, who had our former loanee Chris Whyte at the back, drawing 1-1 but were still unbeaten into October.

There was a story which reported that we had "ripped off Greenwich Borough" when Wright was signed, and they were now living "a hand to mouth existence". Our chairman Noades refuted the claim saying Wright wasn't contracted to them at the time.

Wright was now in the England squad, along with Nigel Martyn emphasising the progress we had made. Hammerings at the likes of Grimsby seem a million miles away. Meanwhile clubs were also after Coppell, Fiorentina were said to be interested, and now Everton. There was better news with Salako and Bright, both signing four-year contracts.

With an international break interfering with our great season, I went with Andy to see West Ham at Bristol City where we had prebooked the Armstrong House B&B. When we got there the owner seemingly didn't like the look of us and now said they were double booked so we went to the less salubrious Crescent Guest House. We went out for the evening and the following morning found Andy's back car window had been smashed, glass was everywhere. The game ended 1-1 in a heated atmosphere. As we stood segregated from the home fans after the game the small constable told a group of West Ham fans, all of which seemed a foot taller and several stone larger, "don't worry lads I'll protect you" to much laughter. Eventually the police let us walk back to the car, but the further Andy and I walked, the less West Ham fans were walking with us, and we suddenly felt very vulnerable after rumours of trouble all day. For no obvious reason we got spooked and sprinted the last few minutes back to the car as if we were escapees from Colditz. Good friend Wags said years later "Nothing good ever happens in Bristol." It wasn't our best trip.

We seem to have upset Liverpool legend Tommy Smith. After we drew at Everton he dismissed us "It shows how weak the league is if Palace are fourth". Hey, Tommy – who won at Villa park?" A good trip, with the £13 coach stopping for beers!

Not only unbeaten to October but to November. Amazing. A fantastic tussle with Wimbledon made sure of that. Drawing 1-1 at half time we turned on the style in the second half with Humphrey stroking in a loose ball, and Gray slamming home from Bright's header. We looked top class, but a superb chip from Fashanu brought them back into it. Bright then added a fourth and we thought that was it, but McGee rounded Martyn and it was a very tense finish, but we held on to win 4-3. A good pick by ITV's "The London Match". As a club everything was very rosy, profits of £1.8 million were staggering after the money troubles of just a few years ago.

It is more famous for ending Arsenal's 49 game unbeaten run, but Old Trafford also ended our 11-game unbeaten start, a tame 2-0 defeat. The optimism that Rob, Duncan, Paul, and I had in the Jolly Angler near Manchester Piccadilly waned after

Webb and Wallace scored within 20 minutes. Not much happened after that. Noades upset their chairman Martin Edwards the following week when he implied that United and Arsenal would escape sanction after a brawl at Highbury "Considering the rough play from Palace in the cup final replay it ill becomes him" moaned Edwards.

We got through a League cup replay at Orient on a chilly night, then faced Arsenal with their legendary back four plus Seaman. I thought it was important not to lose after the defeat at United. It ended 0-0 but was a high-quality game just lacking goalmouth action. We got 28,000 in for that producing record receipts of £228,000. As I watched it, I thought how good life was at Selhurst: A top of the table clash against the Gunners in front of a full house. Got to enjoy the good times whilst you can!

We dominated QPR the following week, the only mystery was how it took so long for us to get a winner, Wright finally scoring from a near post header in front of the Palace end that spread round the sides of the ground. "It was like a home game for us," said Richard Shaw. After our F.A.Cup quarter final defeat eight years earlier I always enjoy winning here. Our goals were our first against QPR since the sixties!

We then enjoyed another highly impressive away win, this time at Southampton. Winning felt routine now! We kindly gave them a chance with a Shaw own goal in the first minute, but we fully deserved a 3-2 win. We are full of pace and confidence up front, and Thorn, Young and Martyn give us such a strong base. Combine that with Gray and Thomas dominating so many games in midfield and it is little wonder we are still 4th. I drove down on my own. After the game I couldn't just not find the car, but I couldn't even find the car park! It took me about an hour to find the multi storey, just before the security guy was going to lock it up for the night. I can be clueless sometimes! In 2001 Keeley Bugg and I were unable to locate my car after a game at Walsall even though it was in the club car park. We went back to the Dell three days later for a League cup game but didn't play anywhere near as well and lost 2-0 with a chilly wind making it that little bit worse.

Alex Dyer left for Charlton. He had seemed a great signing when he arrived if only to stop him roasting our defence playing for Hull. The thought of him combining with Wright, Bright, McGoldrick and Salako seemed exciting and a perfect match but it never worked out for him.

It wasn't a classic, but we beat Coventry despite a scrappy performance. A familiar story began with us getting two up only to let in a goal to set up a tense finish. This was despite Speedie's being harshly sent off, most thought referee Hackett got his red card out because of his reputation. "The finish shouldn't have been such a climax." said a relieved Coppell.

In the pub after the game we chatted over just how fantastic this season had been so far. It was amazing to be third and chasing a spot in Europe. A long way to go and our squad depth is a bit thin but if we were to hang on to third we would qualify for Europe. This season it was the champions qualifying for the European Cup and with Liverpool and Arsenal battling that out we had a chance of getting the only UEFA Cup spot as Liverpool were still banned next season following the Heysel disaster. Never did we think in the dark days at Selhurst in 1985 with crowds about 4,000 and struggling in division two that this ban may affect us! Deep down we all knew it was more likely we would slip down the league but even a top half finish would be great. The main objective for me was to make sure we didn't end up near the relegation zone for a few years.

A few drinks in Victoria increased our confidence for the trip to Chelsea, but we didn't play well and a deflection off Shaw gave them a winner. We were better at home to Luton, winning with Bright scoring from Salako's cross. Hopefully, that gave Salako some relief from the relentless stick he got from Wright and Bright if his service was not to their liking. Once again, we had a tense finish when we should have had the game wrapped up well before the end. I missed the ZDS second round clash with Bristol Rovers to resume my managerial role with our five-a-side team. A victory over Pound Hill Dairies gave us the chance of making the play-offs. This seemed much more important than a ZDS game, but the next round would be much more interesting, rivals Brighton away.

Our 2-0 win at Manchester City was full of class. Maine Road was a wonderful ground, full of atmosphere, and an intimidating place. We had some luck with a first half own goal, but we dominated large patches of the game, and after Young made a superb last-ditch challenge on Heath, Wright wrapped things up. City boss Peter Reid was impressed "They have as good a chance of any of winning the league title. They are very well organised." Wow. Chances of winning the first division.

Like many years we didn't look so great on Boxing Day. We went behind to Sunderland and just couldn't get going. But as is often the case when you're going well we got two late goals to win it. There was drama when Martyn appeared to bring down Rush in the box at the end, but no penalty was given to infuriate Sunderland Manager Smith "That is the most blatant penalty I have seen for a long time." Oh well I thought whilst sipping traditional Boxing Day gin and tonics. I doubt the Sunderland fans, who had such an awful journey during Christmas thought the same, but we did lay on breakfast for their supporters who had to leave at midnight Christmas Day for the lunchtime kick off. Great planning, not that Rob had any sympathy, he had a strong dislike of the Mackems and made this very clear to them as they boarded their coach for the long trip back.

Next was the mighty Liverpool. Memories of the 9-0 defeat and the staggering semi-final win were still in everyone's mind.

Now we were virtually level with them, and the game was chosen for live ITV coverage. This time we showed beyond doubt that if we play at our best we can beat anyone. It wasn't so long ago that good second division teams would outclass us but today we looked better than Liverpool and won with a scrambled goal from Bright just before half time. Wright was superb and the team look so strong particularly in the middle of the pitch with Martyn, Young, Thorn, Thomas, Gray, Wright and Bright. Heading all this was manager Coppell who Noades lauded as "the best boss in the game." We were not favourites for relegation now and were even in the betting for the championship. Those odds lengthened on New Year's Day 1991 with David Platt inspiring Villa to beat us 2-0.

The BBC chose our F.A.Cup tie with Forest to be their live match. They chose poorly. I am never in favour of live matches in the earlier rounds between two top division teams. Surely you want to cover possible upsets which is the whole spirit of the third round. The BBC maybe thought they could rehash the Villa park semi-final in the build up and go on about Brian Clough having never won it. This was a dull goalless affair where I found myself checking the replay dates half an hour in.

We continued our league form with a trip to struggling Sheffield United, this time on a club train with Clubby, Adrian and Brian. They were scrambling for points at the bottom, and it was a physical battle on a bitterly cold day which we nicked with Bright's volley from McGoldrick's cross. Coppell praised referee Pawley "He handled the game superbly and in the spirit of the competitive nature of the match." The result left us in third, and now six points clear of fourth. This means, in view of Liverpool's ban, we have a great chance of finishing there and therefore being in the UEFA cup next season – what fun that would be. Our standing in the game was also boosted with news that Palace were trying to put Selhurst on the international scene should England host the 1998 World Cup.

But planning permission would be needed to boost the capacity to the required, 40,000.

We were poor on 19th January, beaten 3-1 by Norwich who passed us off the pitch in stark contrast to the thrashing we gave them at Carrow Road. "We got what we deserved," said Coppell. He was right. The referee was Alan Gunn, who didn't give us a clear penalty in the Cup final replay. He got a ropy reception.

The Forest replay was always going to be tough. We generally struggled there but with the likes of Pearce, Walker, Hodge, Keane, and Nigel Clough they were a high-quality passing side superbly managed by Brian Clough. This was no different, and our more athletic game was a good contrast to Forest's technical skills. It looked as if we had won when Wright volleyed us ahead on 73 minutes, but a deflection off Shaw got them level, so we went to extra time. Once the formidable Stuart Pearce put them ahead that seemed to be it. With the clock showing just seconds remaining a back pass from Keane was a little short so keeper Crossley came to the edge of the box to clear, he didn't connect well and the ball fell for Salako just inside Forest's half and he sent a superb chip over the backtracking Crossley and over the line. A second replay beckoned. We lost the toss and it'll be another journey to the City Ground. "Good" said Clough. We groaned at the thought of another M1 trip.

This second replay was called off when we were on the M1 for fog. The game was re-arranged for the Saturday but that was postponed due to a frozen pitch. We made yet another trip to Forest on the Monday and once again it was a tight affair with nothing to choose until Forest had a purple patch and slammed in three goals in ten impressive minutes and we were out. A big disappointment as we certainly had a team to get to the later stages again. Palace thought Clough had tried to make a point over the competitiveness of our team by taking Hodge off towards the end to "save him" despite having already used all his subs.

We had made two completed trips to Forest, and two aborted ones over the last ten days so guess where our next league game was. Yep, Forest away. Jay and I travelled up in Paul's car with his Jesus Jones tape to enjoy. It was a grey day with snow coming down as we went past Toddington, Newport Pagnell, Rothersthorpe and Watford Gap services yet again. The game reflected the freezing weather and Martyn made some fine saves to keep us in it early on. We got better in the second half and earned a free kick with four minutes to go from which the superb Eric Young nodded in to put us ahead. Cue pandemonium. The frustrations of all these trips all came out of the Palace end. We drove off glad to finally be away from the relentless "Psycho", "You'll never beat Des Walker" and "You've lost that loving feeling" chants. Revenge was certainly much enjoyed. "Pub?" I asked. "Oh yeah," said Jay.

The freezing weather meant the Spurs home game was off. Then we drew on a bitter afternoon with QPR with snow piled up to the side of the pitch. We lacked the creative touch to get past the impressive Peacock at the back and a lethargic match ended goalless. The game did see Stan Collymore make his debut. Such a shame that he never reached his potential with Palace.

The ZDS rarely caught the public imagination but a tie at Brighton certainly interested us! We dominated it but couldn't score so into extra time we went. We won with Bright and Wright scoring, and a Seagull friend of Jay Sisley's said it was the biggest frenzy of celebration he'd ever seen in the away end. The atmosphere after the game walking back to the station was very edgy, particularly with helicopters on hand to try and spot any trouble.

We were outclassed at Arsenal, simple as that, and they got two goals in each half for a comprehensive victory.

We were now effectively in the quarter final of the ZDS cup and faced Luton. I was playing five a side, but my Dad went and said Palace were patchy. We got through 3-1. Strangely a ginger cat got onto the pitch, Capital Gold's Johnathan Pearce described it as "The fastest thing we've seen all night".

We produced a tired looking effort at Coventry in cold rainy weather and lost 3-1. I drove and was somehow talked into going via WBA both ways by Andy so he could see West Ham get a draw. Why, as was more logical, he didn't drive and drop me off remains a mystery. Even so the excitement on going on the new M40 was nearly too much to handle. On the way home we heard we had signed left back Paul Bodin for £550,000, with Shaw in very decent form Coppell even admitted we didn't need him.

We drew the area final first leg of the ZDS at Norwich, then beat Southampton in a typical let's get two up and then create tension by letting a late goal in style. The crowd was only 14,529 which was disappointing considering we are third in the league. The following week we beat Derby. Guess what? We got two goals up and let in a late goal – can we ever relax at Selhurst? I thought it a warning for next season as these very narrow wins could so easily have been draws then so many points would be lost. But, hey, we are still third which was simply brilliant.

We made Wembley for the second season in a row with a comfortable win at Selhurst over Norwich and we will play Everton in the final of the ZDS Cup. We produced one of our best home performances of the season in a very positive atmosphere. With the club set to rake in about £500,000 and us getting a great day out this doesn't seem such a Micky Mouse cup any more particularly to a club where two finals in two seasons were beyond a pipedream a few seasons ago. A point Coppell emphasised "It's a thank you to the 5,000 that were coming in my first season".

The biggest threat to us finishing third, and so qualifying for the UEFA cup, were Leeds in fourth who had couple of games in hand so it was a big game at Elland Road. I travelled up with Brian, Rob Mukerji and Dave Lewis all of whom had started displaying their skills in our new five-a-side B team. The previous Tuesday the B's had three big lads playing, Andy Wagon, Neil Witherow and John Bugg and little pacy Pete up front. In the first half Pete got kicked all over the place but at half time I heard their captain tell the rest of the team "lay off the little bloke, I don't fancy mixing it with the other three." In the second half they didn't get near Pete and he scored a hat-trick to win us the game.

The slightly more higher profile game at Leeds started well with the ball deflecting of Mel Sterland straight to Wright to put us ahead. Gary Speed equalised by half time and during the break we agreed a dull eventless second half would be great for our European hopes. Leeds did have more of the second half, but with a minute left Wright broke down the right and he squared it for Salako to score in front of the home kop end. A great win.

It was back to the queues for ZDS final tickets the next day but with 30,000 available I decided not to get up too early. It may well be that a good few beers on the trip back from Leeds had some impact on that decision.

We lost at Sunderland to a dubious offside decision for their winner, then to Manchester City at home 3-1 with Niall Quinn causing more trouble to the formidable Thorn and Young that anyone else had, scoring a hattrick. Coppell admitted what many thought "Maybe our minds were on the Zenith Cup final."

It may not be the greatest cup competition ever staged but we were promised a great day out at Wembley. For starters it would avoid all the corporate people taking up so many tickets that could go to supporters. We had 32,000 for this one with some going on the 60 coaches many decked out in red and blue. Noades was also pleased. More money in our coffers to give us a slight advantage yet again in the transfer market after the Cup and Play-offs finals in recent years. The extra money will mean the financial loss of losing Charlton as ground sharers will be softened. The papers built the game up, with Scottish striker Andy Gray lauding Coppell as someone that could rival the legend of Brian Clough, plus the opportunities for the likes of Wright, Bright, Thomas, Gray and Salako to remind England manager Graham Taylor that they could play on the big stage.

I got the 11.21 with Andy (who I had travelled to the glamour of Port Vale with the previous day to see a West Ham victory) and met the usual suspects at Victoria. We struggled to get a pre-game drink in as all the pubs were packed with Palace fans. We got into the ground and there was no doubt there was an air of confidence that after last season that this was our time at Wembley. The first half was dull, and the start of the second half not much better but a sterile game was enlivened when Thomas stooped in to score from a near post corner, a tactic we regularly employed with success. We celebrated wildly but looked up to see Warzycha equalise straight away thanks to some shoddy marking. From then the game was fantastic, both teams attacking like it was basketball and two fine keepers Southall and Martyn making excellent saves. Neither were beaten as we went into extra time. Ten minutes into that Wright sprinted through the Everton defence and I just knew he would score and was celebrating long before he rolled the ball into the net. I hoped we would hold on, but we did more than that. Salako looped a header over Southall and the celebrations really started and Wright's slickly taken fourth was the icing on the cake. It wasn't the F.A.Cup but it was an emotional moment when Geoff Thomas went up to lift the ZDS cup whilst Southall got a sulk on and sat leaning against the post. Obviously we celebrated back at Baker Street where we did manage to get a few drinks in thinking how wonderful these times were, third in the first division and a cup win after all those years of desperate struggle. "The Eagle has landed" and "A Wright old Palace Knees-up" were typical morning headlines.

Meanwhile there was some change afoot. An elite Premier League was said to be closer than ever with plans for an 18-club division being approved for 1992-93. Although we were third and looking so strong, it wasn't lost on me that would mean more teams being relegated over the next couple of seasons. Meanwhile Palace announced a £2m sponsorship deal with Crawley computer company, Tulip and we had plans to build a 9,100-capacity stand at the Holmesdale Road end.

I made a traditional support-the-opposition trip to the Goldstone Ground, but that went badly as Andy was furious that West Ham lost to a scrappy goal. Our next game was a dull draw with Aston Villa although we did parade the ZDS cup at half time. There was good news from Elland Road, Leeds who had been closing the gap on us, were beaten 5-4 by Liverpool so we were four points clear of fourth.

We extended that gap with a tight 1-0 over Spurs with Young scoring early in a cracking atmosphere, whilst Leeds lost at QPR. Eric "The Ninja" Young had turned out to be a superb signing and he had formed a perfect partnership with Thorn so much so that many in the media considered them the best pairing in the league, so we let Gary O'Reilly leave for Birmingham on loan. We'd also seen the debut of Paul Bodin at left back, and Simon Osborne who looked tiny but showed plenty of promise. Alternative left back Mark Dennis had been sacked during the week for a "breach of discipline" the details of which were unclear. This may explain why Bodin was brought in.

With third place a near certainty, we got some disastrous news. The understanding all season had been that English clubs would get two spaces in Europe. One would be for the league champions in the European Cup, the other would be for the UEFA Cup for the second placed team. However, as

Liverpool were to have a further one-year ban following Heysel that meant the third-place team, so probably Palace, would take that spot. It was now announced that the Liverpool ban had been cancelled and so they, not us, would have the UEFA spot. Noades, who later threatened to sue, was furious "Here we go again, one rule for the big, one rule for the rest. It is a backstabbing decision. What is the point in changing the rules in April, it is a terrible blow." Meanwhile Coppell curiously called the FA "A load of chocolate solders." Surely they could have found a spot for both Liverpool and us. Our cause was not helped as four UEFA places went to East Germany, which no longer existed. Some feared that without European football some of our players may be tempted to leave.

We played Everton on a freezing late April day with occasional blizzards. It was a disappointing game the "highlight" being Martin Keown's sending off for elbowing Young, who would miss the rest of the season as a result. With Wright struggling for form, we rarely looked like getting a winner.

We then had to go to Liverpool with no Thorn, Young, Gray, Bright or Barber so it was not looking too hopeful. "They'll get nine again" Andy warned. On the way up we did fear he could be right as we read through the range of fanzines Dave had brought with him. Coppell blooded young Gareth Southgate who did a superb job marking Rush as a partner to Shaw and employed McGoldrick as a sweeper. The tactic was deemed a success, but we still lost 3-0 despite never ending chants of "Stevie Coppell's red n blue army" echoing round Anfield. The club train got us home after the tube had stopped operating so with no taxis or buses about, we walked back to Victoria and I got home at 3am, luckily I had someone to follow.

Andy had been getting chirpier as the season went on with West Ham certainties to get promotion. We had a cracking weekend in Blackpool to see them "win to clinch the championship" at Blackburn. Well, according to Andy. They lost 3-1. I tried not to giggle. My giggling didn't get any less when Andy suffered a bit of Delhi belly after a curry the night before. To say strange noises were coming out of his toilet cubicle in the Ewood Park away end would be an understatement much to the merriment of those outside. I giggled further when I found Palace's reserves had beaten West Ham reserves 11-0. "You thought nine was bad" I told him.

We welcomed back Thorn at Wimbledon who we thrashed with a hat-trick from Wright who found his form again and finished the game with a superb chip from near the half-way line. We were brilliant in the second half, after a dull first period. It was later announced that Wimbledon would be replacing Charlton as our lodgers, all very useful income I thought, although many others didn't like the idea.

This memorable season finished in a carnival like atmosphere as we beat Manchester United 3-0. A big crowd on a bright day saw keeper Walsh gift Wright our first, and Salako added two second half goals.

We finished third. A fantastic achievement that nobody thought remotely possible back in August. Our top scorer was Ian Wright with 25, but he was pipped as my player of the season by Eric Young. We had four players making all 52 appearances – Humphrey, Martyn, Thomas, and Wright.

Selhurst finished the season with a strange cricket match. Unsurprisingly that doesn't quite work on a football pitch. During this we discussed the need to strengthen our squad still further, but it was difficult to see who we could replace to get stronger! No quality striker would want to be on the bench behind Wright and Bright and much the same could be said about most other areas of the team. The days of it being a squad game were still some way off.

The big question for us was can we build on this and somehow match or even better this season, or would this turn out to be the pinnacle of this era?

Chapter 11: 1991/92 – Start of the slide.

Except for poor cup runs last season was a dream. We would turn up at almost any club in the country and be confident that we could win, and invariably we did, finishing third. A controversial decision not to allow us into Europe when the Liverpool ban was lifted was the only disappointment.

Some league wins though were very tight and it wasn't lost on us that if results just went the other way, through worse luck or form, we could slip well down the table. We hoped that some quality signings could be attracted following our lofty league position to consolidate us in the top half of the league at least.

Some things didn't change. For the 43rd consecutive summer we were linked with Sunderland's Gary Bennett, but more encouragingly with high class Derby striker Dean Saunders plus Mark Walters, Rod Wallace, and Franz Carr all of which would have added to our squad. Instead we were left unexcited by signing two low key defenders, Lee Sinnott for £350,000 from Bradford and Chris Coleman for an initial £275,000 from Swansea. Neither could be described as players likely to lift us even higher or maintain our position of last year. Many felt we had missed a rare opportunity for our club to compete at the top end of the market as we hadn't taken advantage of our current standing in the league.

We had lost a few decent players over the summer. Firstly Phil Barber joined Millwall for £125,000, then Gary O'Reilly presumably had some kind of brain freeze and chose to re-join Brighton on a free transfer whilst wholehearted striker Garry Thompson went to QPR for £100,000. Ian Branfoot also left, to become Southampton manager. There were rumours that Andy Gray was unhappy again which was worrying with Chelsea lining up a bid. At least we didn't lose any key players despite Arsenal's interest in Thomas, Liverpool enquiring about Salako, and Everton doing the same about Wright. We were quoted at 20/1 to win the top division. How times have changed!

Our quality was emphasised with Thomas, Wright and Salako all playing in the same game for England on a trip to New Zealand. Martyn was often in squads to and occasionally Gray. Staggering to have five involved for a club of our stature and I was delighted we had kept them all over the summer.

All the usual crew joined me for Palace's 6-0 friendly win at my hometown team Crawley, then in the Beazer Homes league. This was followed by the usual easy wins on a Swedish tour, victory over Millwall, and a defeat at Fulham. We also played in the "Costa Verde" tournament beating Levski 3-1 and drawing with Sporting Gijon. Andy and I went to the Makita tournament at Highbury. He wasn't happy when the 'ammers lost 6-1 to Sampdoria on the Saturday. "We'll see you in September" I said to Andy totally confident that we would smash them out of sight.

Dad and I were a couple of days away from taking up our seats once again in Row 35 of the Arthur Wait when our opener against Leeds was called off as the creation of new executive boxes and the police control room were unfinished. Leeds were not impressed, manager Wilkinson called it "a disgrace."

Instead, we kicked off with a trip to Manchester City where we played very well but lost an ill-tempered game 3-2 thanks to conceding a late spot kick which Coppell called a "home" penalty. The £20 inter-city allowed me to lose in some comfort at cards but winning our predictascore got my money back. The inclusive bus was a welcome addition, but not so much after the game when on a very muggy day we had to wait on it for ages watching City fans gleefully pointing the score out as they walked on by. A fun trip ended with drinks in Victoria Station concourse, as we couldn't get in the pubs outside as Dave had a football shirt on which apparently meant he was going to create a riot at a drop of a hat.

Next up was a sensational evening game against Wimbledon, a fitting way to open the new executive boxes. From start to finish it was a Selhurst classic. We had hit the post before Fashanu put them ahead. This was followed by Martyn being sent off by David Elleray for violent conduct leaving Salako as makeshift keeper. It always added to the fun to see an outfield player in goal, shame that never happens these days. Despite being down to ten men Palace were excellent and Bright equalised, then on the stroke of half time Terry Phelan handled on the line and was sent off and Gray slammed home the penalty. 2-1 up at half time but with a very dodgy keeper, so what could possibly go wrong? Wright put us further head, and when they had Ryan sent off for a second booking the game looked won. But obviously Palace were Palace and Earle made it 3-2 with three minutes left to leave the crowd very nervy. With the referee looking at his watch Wimbledon got a last-minute corner, and a great cross was met by Cork and Salako incredibly made a world class save to make sure we got the points. Cracking game!

Glyn Hodges put Sheffield United ahead on the Saturday with a great shot into the top corner at the Holmesdale end, but we turned it on in the last ten minutes with Thomas equalising then I enjoyed Wright's late winner so much I managed to get myself to the front of the stand 34 steps down. We got three more points with Wright getting an early winner at Aston Villa. We had paid £10 for seats in advance which were only £9.50 on the day and were told we could get a refund, but that never materialised. We nearly passed out in a state of shock on the trip home as Radio Five gave us some praise. Wonders will never cease.

With the club having made such progress - promotion, cup final, ZDS victory and a good start again crowds were disappointing. Noades was clearly concerned "Gates of 15,000 will not be enough to keep our best players. We must get to 20,000".

Noades hit the papers for the wrong reasons with headlines such as "Palace TV race fury" and "Noades in peace talks with his players." This related to the Channel Four Critical Eye documentary "Great Britain United". On it Noades was reported to have said black stars needed the support of hard-working whites to carry them through the English winter. Andy Gray came to the defence of Noades "There is no way Ron is racist and all this talk of trouble at the club is utter rubbish." Channel four refused to pull the plug on the show and confirmed "Mr Noades doesn't come out of it too well" but Ron defended himself by saying he was talking about black players in the early days. Luther Blissett weighed in saying black Palace players should walk out, and Ian Wright was clearly unhappy and was said to be reporting Noades to the Race Relations Board.

We headed to Everton next and were only allocated the £8.50 seats high behind the goal, but they gave a fine view of a lively 2-2 draw. We had taken the lead from a penalty, which I celebrated with a little too much gusto slamming my knee into Robbie's seat which made the wait for the 6.40pm train home none too comfortable. Programme sellers were also not particularly willing to give accurate change, Robbie made a profit on his transaction, Dave queried why change of only 50p was forthcoming for his £20, and I was nearly charged £6.50 for one I lost anyway after a few gin and tonics. Our team was again embroiled in a "physical game". It just looked competitive to me, but the papers seem to have a bit of an agenda on us. The report in the Sun was particularly harsh, so I wrote a letter to the Sports Editor telling them to get off our case.

We didn't turn up against Arsenal, getting beat 4-1 at home in front of 24,000 although the crowd looked considerably more. Coppell was unimpressed "It was embarrassing, and we were given a lesson." If the race incident had any impact, we'll never know but wife Novello wearing a top saying "My husband is not a racist" drew further attention to this ugly affair. Hopefully, a public apology from Noades will put it to bed.

A big one for me was West Ham, a clash against best mate Andy's team. I wanted to show him just how good we were, I didn't just want to win I wanted to thrash them even though we were missing Martyn and Gray. The crowd looked huge and we were perplexed at the 21,363 attendance figure, some had their suspicions why this figure was so low despite the gates being shut well before kick-off. My Dad had kindly moved along just a few seats so I could sit next to Andy for this one and we started well with Salako putting us ahead during an early scramble and were clearly the better team up to half time. Then disaster as Mitchel Thomas found space in the box and headed past Suckling, then two minutes later a long punt from Miklosko struck Morley's shin and the ball slid agonisingly past the advancing Suckling into an open net. I was now getting relentless digs in the ribs from Andy. Wright scored from close range to make it 2-2. I hardly celebrated. This needed to be a comfortable win boys!! With 15 minutes to go the hopeless ex Seagull Mike Small found space behind Eric Young and headed a winner. I couldn't believe it. We had lost 3-2. A disaster. I knew I would hear all about this right up until we played again - and I wasn't disappointed.

Next up was Oldham on the £20 train with Robbie, Paul, and Dave. We met Duncan, Iain and QPR sponsored walker Paul for another fun trip. We stood in the uncovered windswept corner terrace and watched a way more convincing performance which was very welcome after consecutive home defeats. We had a few beers watching the now infamous Eubank v Watson boxing in Victoria all feeling confident that Palace would press on from this excellent 3-2 away win.

As I got home, I put Ceefax on to see how my lower league team, Hartlepool, got on. I never found out. My eyes were stunned at the main football headline "Wright agrees £2.5m Arsenal move." I couldn't believe it. Ian was fundamental to our club and his enthusiasm had helped transform us from being a very average second division team to one of the best in the country. He was irreplaceable, and today I had seen his last goal and appearance for us. Arsenal were a top team so I understand why he would be interested in a move to them. However, many thought the decision to deny us that UEFA cup spot last season had come home to roost, and the race incident with Noades could have been a factor. Good friend Neil Witherow described it recently as a "seismic moment." If felt that way.

There were also talk that Bright could leave, possibly in a deal to bring John Fashanu to Selhurst. Our team sounded on the verge of break up and I was worried. Pictures of Wright in an Arsenal top did little to cheer me up.

The big question was how to move forward from this. We still had some good players and with money to spend we should be OK. The rumour mill suggested three forwards were on our radar. Firstly, Alan Shearer a very promising striker at Southampton but apparently he didn't fancy his next move being to Selhurst. Secondly, Brian Deane an awkward big striker with pace too. Or thirdly, Marco Gabbiadini, who had a good goalscoring record at Sunderland. There was even speculation we would get two of them, but it wasn't clear if this meant Bright would leave too. Eventually the incomer was Gabbiandini, aged 23, for £1.8m who said on signing "Ian is a hard act to follow, but I don't feel any extra pressure." Really? Everyone knew he would have to hit the ground running and I worried he would lack the pace to have the impact of Wright but frankly anyone would have seemed a downgrade at the time. It was a shame nobody realised a potential answer was already at the club, Stan Collymore. Despite trying to convince ourselves differently there was no doubt Wright's departure felt like an and of an era and I worried how far we would fall, particularly if Gabbiadini wasn't a success, to mid-table? Or worse?

Despite all this Paul, Dave and I went on the seven-hour coach trip to Hartlepool for a League cup tie. A cold September night with one side of the ground a work site did little to raise the spirits and a 1-1 draw was uninspiring. There were people shouting at Noades that his comments had a cost us Wright, and rumours persisted that our goal scorer Bright, and Thomas, could be off too so not the most joyous of trips. Many thought chicken and chips in a pub nearby on the way up was the highlight. I got home at 3.40am so arrived at work two hours late. I was still at working at TACA so nobody cared.

Our first home game post Wright started badly being two down to QPR halfway through the second half. The disillusionment was palpable. Bright gave us hope and then Collymore came on as sub to replace Osborne and whilst his passing was poor, he did grab an equaliser. Meanwhile Wright scored a hat-trick on his Arsenal debut. A few days later we beat second placed Leeds with Thorn and Young resuming their formidable partnership and we won with an injury time winner from Bright, who was proving Wright's departure was not affecting his goalscoring ability. But even in the seconds remaining Batty nearly grabbed an even later equaliser with a clever chip. Gabbiadini made his debut and had a decent game and nearly scored with a blistering first half volley. Sadly, the evening was significantly tarnished with Salako picking up what looked like a very bad knee injury so that's more pace that will be lost up front. However, we were 7th which was still very good.

I had a weekend in Glossop for the Sheffield Wednesday trip with Ian, Paul, Duncan and Pauly which involved a free college disco, and the offer of using a "bong". A filter device with a tube. Beer was poured in one end and flowed down the tube directly into your mouth. The game, seen in a haze after the previous night, was hopeless. We lost 4-1 with centre back Sinnott at left back and no recognised winger. Coppell though was more upset at the coverage of Salako's injury on Saint & Greavsie calling the footage being shown of his leg bending backwards "to be in remarkably bad taste". He could be out for 18 months.

After a slow start we slaughtered Hartlepool 6-1 in the League cup with Gabbiadini scoring his first, whilst his brother was on the other team. I went with Andy to see Barnet beat York, but it was just an excuse for some beers in London. Whilst having these we picked up a Sunday paper which reported we were to sign winger Paul Mortimer for £500,000 from Villa. At 23 he seemed a good acquisition in view of Salako's injury. Andy also joined Rob in my car for a trip to Coventry when Bright and Gabbiadini gave us three more points. After the game it was announced that Steve Harrison would be joining Palace as a coach.

Two low key home games followed, a win over Southend as we began our defence of the ZDS, and a tedious 0-0 with Chelsea. A trip to Birmingham was next in the League cup. We put in a very poor performance and lost Thorn to injury. Sturridge then gave them a lead when Martyn and Humphrey allowed a cross to evade them. There looked to be no chance of an equaliser, but we got out of jail when Gray latched onto a long ball and rounded the keeper to earn us a replay. Cue manic celebrations on the corner terrace and a cheery coach journey home. Spirits had also been high on the way there with many using the kia orange trick of injecting vodka/gin into the foil to liven up the supposedly alcohol-free journey. The friendly steward lady seemed very surprised that many were a little wobbly when we arrived at St. Andrews.

Coppell admitted before the trip to Anfield that he was still haunted by the 9-0 two seasons ago and having lost there 3-0 in the best season in the club's history we travelled with little optimism. The ground greeted us with the sobering Hillsborough plaque, but once in the ground the cheerful red and blue balloons were out. We were one down at half time, but Gabbiadini then had his finest moment in a Palace shirt finishing off a fine flowing move to silence the Kop. Then

Thomas got a winner from Rodgers cross to complete one of the best wins in the club's history. Much was made of Liverpool being without Barnes, Whelan, and Wright. We had players missing too but as the smaller team that, as ever, wasn't mentioned. After the last two seasons it was a very satisfying win. The game was also Alan Pardew's last, he joined Charlton. "He's not that bad surely," said Paul.

We then beat Southampton to get up to 5th, Mortimer was ineffective, and Shearer missed their best chances. I told my Dad it was lucky we didn't sign him. Gray was quiet as well with Coppell blaming his midweek trip to Poland with England. The weekend saw further transfer speculation with Bright's future uncertain, and a £1m bid being lined up for Wimbledon left back Terry Phelan.

In midweek we were lucky not to lose to Birmingham in the League cup replay. Only a 116th minute equaliser got us a second replay. I loved the days of multiple replays, the individual battles often got more niggly which added to the interest.

In the league we headed to Forest and got hammered 5-1 with Thomas admitting "We had no idea went wrong" and the team got a roasting from Coppell. The only good news was Dave had taken advantage of a Boots voucher system giving away free inter-city tickets, so we paid only £8.50 to see our thrashing but at least we met Duncan for a few beers in the King John pub. In there I was talking Dave through our 5-0 defeat at the end of the 1979/80 season, and he said it was only 4-0. Two rules in life, don't mix wine and beer and second don't bet against Dave on football stuff. He was right. We once met John Burridge on a train, he even corrected him over a result in 1978, in a match Budgie played in.

We won at QPR in the ZDS, but I missed it as we had a critical five-a-side match. I listened to the enthusiastic commentary from Jonathan Pearce on Capital Gold. Many current radio commentators could learn from him, describing the match in detail and not getting side-tracked. The game was memorable largely because Nigel Martyn had a rare poor game, but we still won 3-2.

Manchester United hadn't won the league since 1967 and despite Mortimer putting us ahead, they showed why they are favourites for it this season. Two quick second half goals gave them a convincing 3-1 win to narrow the gap on Leeds who were top. It was not lost on us that we finished a place above Leeds in third last season and whilst we brought a couple of lower league defenders they splashed out on Eric Cantona, Rod Wallace, and Tony Dorigo,

We finally got past Birmingham in the League cup, but it was still very tight. Worryingly Gabbiadini looks off the boil. Just one goal in nine and he was clearly upset at being replaced by Collymore.

On my 25th birthday Andy and I stayed over in Norwich at the bargain Earlham Guest House. The game was end to end but a last-minute Newman tap in got Norwich a 3-3 draw. I was disappointed but an excellent pub crawl, wins on fruit machines, and games of pool meant all was good in the world again. Delia Smith went up in my estimation though in her match report "If fan volume was anything to go by Palace would be top of the league."

We went out to Chelsea in the ZDS, then Gray got us a win at Swindon to take us to the League cup quarter finals. There was always a good atmosphere there, although there "give us a S, give us a…Wubble U…" chant got on my nerves. It was a surprise to nobody that we drew Forest, yet again, in the next round.

Gabbiadini was struggling and was becoming known as "Mr Average". It was a tough gig to take over from Wright and he just wasn't scoring or contributing much. His style didn't fit with us and it was becoming a worry particularly as there were relentless reports about Bright being unsettled too. Marco again struggled at Spurs with goals from Walsh and Lineker giving them a 2-1 win. We were missing both Thorn and Young and it showed. Life got better for Gabbiadini as he scored at Wimbledon in a 1-1 draw in a poor game that may ease the reported dressing room unrest at his efforts. He got another as well at Sheffield United in a draw.

We started 1992 with a win over Notts County, with only 14,202 showing up and Gabbiadini scoring again. County looked a good team, and I always had a soft spot for them. The disappointing attendances did worry Noades "Disgraceful. We now have the worst of both worlds, low crowds and low prices." He was unhappy at the criticism the club was receiving and that people still weren't coming "I am sorry we have under achieved. Last year we were third in the first division and won the ZDS. I never realised Palace had done so well before. If someone had told me I would have understood all the slagging off."

We travelled to Leicester in the FA Cup but lost to a last-minute Richard Smith goal and had Young sent off for the second time in a month. I missed this to see Crawley at Palace's rivals Brighton. A big crowd but a disappointing 5-0 defeat during which the Seagull fans chanted "You're going out with the Palace." Andy asked if I could hear that.

Playing Nottingham Forest in cups was becoming so inevitable, and so were the outcomes. Once again, we deserved a win at home and looked like we had it with a Des Walker own goal, but a scrambled 86th minute equaliser stabbed in by Clough was gutting to everyone. At the final whistle we just knew what would happen at the City ground as I kicked the seat in front of me in frustration. The replay was indeed lost a month later, Bright put us ahead after 34 minutes then Forest produced ten minutes of brilliance and were 3-1 up by half time. We ended up losing 4-2 with David Whyte scoring his first goal for us but Sheringham getting a hattrick for them.

League form was starting to stagnate. We drew 1-1 with Manchester City with Keith Curle equalising for them on a gloomy afternoon with a late penalty given very softly for an alleged push by Young on Quinn. Even Peter Reid gave reporters a wry grin knowing they had been lucky. Bright had at least broken a run of 18 matches without a goal. Coppell didn't speak to the media but had made his views on the penalty known to referee Wiseman. He was later fined £1,500 which didn't please him "I see Boris Becker was fined $300 for abusing a line judge, whilst I'm fined an amount just pulled out of a hat". The player Coppell had said we didn't really need when he was signed, Paul Bodin, left for Swindon for £225,000.

Assistant manager Alan Smith made it clear that he didn't think Gabbiadini had been great value for money "There should be a gap between £1m plus players and young players coming through from the youth team." It did not sound like Marco was impressing. He did play at top of the table Leeds where Thomas scored in an encouraging 1-1 draw. Gabbiadini was substituted at Elland Road and it was to be his last game for the club, he moved to Derby for £1.2 million. Therefore, we lost £600,000 in just a few months. It seemed the club were willing to give youngsters David Whyte or Jamie Moralee an opportunity in place of a player we had signed to replace a legend. It was always going to be tough, but the "Mr Average" tag summed him up for me. More disturbing was Andy Gray's row with Coppell. "I'll kick you out. Coppell fury over rebel star" the papers reported.

Noades would have been disheartened again by a 13,818 crowd at home to Coventry, a dire affair that we lost 1-0. Whyte partnered Bright but, as my Dad said, he didn't want the responsibility of shooting but was very skilful. The day ended with Gray being booed at the end, it was all very ugly and worrying.

Andy joined me for the trip to Chelsea, where we were considered a category A team, so we had to pay £9 for the terrace. Whyte looked very promising, putting us ahead and dazzling us with some neat footwork giving us hope that he could form a good partnership with Bright. Sadly, Cascarino got a late equaliser. We joined Paul, Robbie, Jay and Dave in the Globe and the Allsop Arms in Baker Street before a few more in Victoria. Andy, as he always did, fell asleep on the 11.21 train home. When this happens he drops his newspapers all over the floor resulting in disapproving looks towards us. As I looked down and picked them up there were reports of Coppell calling Gray a "misery, just after signing a lucrative new contract". It didn't bode well.

My Dad joined us for the trip to Tottenham but with Gray not in the team there wasn't a great deal of enthusiasm. However with Whyte lively again we won with a late goal from McGoldrick but we were thankful, as ever, to have Martyn in goal. On the walk back to the station Spurs fans were very complimentary about Thomas, comments like "just who we need" were common. I hope you don't get him I thought. The club thought the same and were offering him a five-year contract. Two departures followed, both were so valuable in our promotion year - Perry Suckling and Jeff Hopkins.

The club were keen to build a new 9,200 capacity stand at the Holmesdale Road end. In view of the post Hillsborough Taylor report this is certain to be built, but we need to start building it this summer if we are to get a significant grant. It seems the plan to convert the National Sports Stadium into a 35,000-capacity ground are shelved. Noades was keen to avoid conflict with the fans over the funding the stand noting the division the ill-fated bond scheme had caused at West Ham. "I don't want to tell them what we are going to do but get their support." It seemed this support would be partly financial but as supporters club secretary Chris Plummer said, "I can't see many putting up money unless they get value back". The main idea was to offer long-term season tickets.

Palace travelled to Manchester United on 22 February, but as I missed out on a ticket I went to Hillsborough to see Andy's West Ham lose to Sheffield Wednesday. We got back and dashed to the Tavern on the Green pub in Crawley and bumped into a Palace fan who had been to Old Trafford and said we played well in a 2-0 defeat. Sadly, I thought it would be fine to drink my usual number of pints but in less time. I realised in the morning that this assumption was deeply flawed.

We played OK against Luton in front of only 12,000 and deservedly led through Bright but we slowly went downhill. Brian Stein won a penalty for falling over the ball and it ended 1-1. We were lacking in any creativity and were said to be lining up a £2.5m bid for Brian Deane. We could certainly do with a boost.

Andy Gray's inevitable departure finally took place. He joined Tottenham initially on loan then for £750,000. A sad departure: he has been a brilliant player for us and will be another monumental loss.

More worrying headlines then appeared "Fraud Squad probes £1m soccer lottery. Palace chief Noades to meet cops" Reports did say that Noades was not a suspect, and the story promptly disappeared.

Back on the pitch we ended February with a cracker against Norwich at Selhurst. Norwich passed us off the pitch in the first half and led 4-2 at the break. Bright pulled one back and in the second half we put Norwich under pressure and, although we lost, most were happy to have seen such an entertaining game. At the back of my mind I thought we would have won a game like that last season. We drew with Forest in the league the following Tuesday, again in front of a disappointing 12,000 crowd. "At least there isn't a replay," said Paul.

A forum for members was held the following day, it started in a critical and rather toxic atmosphere but eventually Noades, Coppell and Smith talked entertainingly about all the issues this season. This included details of a confrontation between Gray and Gabbiadini which is also mentioned in Mark Bright's excellent book "My Story". Noades said of Gabbiadini "We did a brilliant deal selling Marco. Derby have the problem now."

We sat in the low dingy seated terrace at Luton and saw us draw 1-1. Most of our crowd spent their time giving Brian Stein grief for his dive at Selhurst ten days previously. At Southampton we were inept losing 1-0, Jamie Moralee got his chance but struggled. In effect our replacement for Wright was now a choice of youngsters or makeshift Chris Coleman, so we surely needed another quality striker. Dean Holdsworth was the latest link, but I thought he was too slow for us.

There was some curious news when it turned out Selhurst Park was being planned as a venue for Euro 96. It seemed a long way off, but the FA had snubbed Highbury in favour of our ground as they wanted one south of the river.

We then faced Liverpool and incredibly completed the double over them thanks to Eric "Ninja" Young scrambling in a winner just before half time. We had endured many mediocre games at Selhurst this season, but this was back to the blood and thunder stuff with Coleman proving to be a handful as a makeshift centre forward.

Trev, James, Paul, and I all enjoyed the FA Youth Cup Semi-final at Wimbledon, it ended 3-3 with Palace going through on aggregate and we will face Manchester United in the final who could include regular first teamer Ryan Giggs. Sounds a challenge! It was then back to mediocrity, a turgid 0-0 against Villa.

A trip in Trev's car to Notts County seemed to give us a good chance to move up a couple of places as they were looking doomed to relegation. We were shocking in the first half though. Dave and his mate Dave "Cantona" Bennett and I all agreed this was a lost cause. They looked like a team desperate for points, and we didn't, and we were 2-1 down. Thankfully County lost their way after the break, and with Thomas taking a grip on the game in midfield Bright levelled, and Mortimer's winner meant we took the points to complete a great comeback.

Dave Bennett joined our five a side team in the summer. Before one match the opposition asked if a young lad played could we go easy with tackles on him as he was quite ill. We all agreed and encouraged him to play. Dave had been in the changing room during this chat and noticed the same lad was wearing a Man United top, not his favourite team. Being an uncompromising defender two minutes in Dave sent the lad flying with a "robust" challenge which made us all wince. Somehow no harm was done!

The Everton home game was billed as a bit of a grudge match. There had been the ZDS final, Young's injury at Keown's hands, and the general opinion on Merseyside that Palace were an over-physical team. The first half belied that feeling of animosity completely as it meandered along at friendly pace. We upped our game in the second half and Coleman, and a Bright penalty, got us the points to take us to 7th. Peter Beagrie had "scored" a fine curling free kick, but referee Bailey disallowed it, Everton were not impressed. A bit of justice for Thorn's sending off at Goodison I thought, so tough.

We suffered our traditional thrashing at Arsenal on the first proper day of spring but at least Wright didn't score. David Seaman had a rare shaky game for them, so we chanted "Scotland's number one" at him which made him grin. A large group of us went for beers in Baker Street's Allsop Arms and found a football computer game where a league and cup were promptly organised. Rob won the double, I did beat him later in the evening, but he blamed his 10th pint for his loss of form. On the way home I stayed awake on the train by reading that Andy Cole was subject of two bids from Bristol City, and us.

A dull 0-0 with Oldham followed in front of only 12,267, I spent most the game looking at the new and good value season ticket prices. Mark Bright felt a need to refresh the squad "I can't see us picking up a trophy without adding to the squad as we have lost internationals Wright, Gray and Salako to either transfer or injury." Most agreed and hoped the money was there to do so.

Andy had long given up hope of his 'ammers staying up this season, and they gifted us three points at the Boleyn with a dire performance typified by right back Tim Breaker simply passing it to Bright in front of goal, as I watched on from Andy's Dad's season ticket seat. Coleman added a second and it was a walk in the park as the fans deserted the ground well before the final whistle. I, of course, made Andy well aware of our victory - but I was disappointed that we wouldn't be playing each other next season.

Sheffield Wednesday had a glimmer of hope of winning the league when they came to Selhurst for the final home game of the season. They were very impressive in the first half and Paul Williams gave them a deserved lead from Sheridan's cross, but a late lobbed equaliser from Bright gave us a deserved point.

The last game at QPR was dull. We had Martyn injured so we got Neil Sullivan on loan for a game, plus we gave young Moralee a go up front. We lost to a first half Humphrey own goal on an ill-tempered afternoon. There was even bad feeling amongst Palace fans when friend Phil had his hat stolen, and Jay had words with someone who pushed Robbie over to complete a forgettable day.

My seasonal stats showed classy Mark Bright led our appearances list with 54 and was comfortably the top goal scorer with 22. Despite that my player of the season was Gray despite all that had happened. Average crowds were 2,000 down on last season which was disappointing as we had just enjoyed the two highest finishes in the club's history.

Over a few beers we knew this season hadn't been great despite finishing 10th which was still very impressive. After the heights of last season it did feel we had taken a back step having lost two of our gold chip players in Wright and Gray, plus Salako to injury, and replacements unsurprisingly not being up to their standard. Some young players, such as Simon Rodger and Gareth Southgate, looked decent but we knew we surely needed some established players to replace the internationals who had left to at least maintain our place in midtable.

Chapter 12: 1992/93 – One more point.

We were no longer in the First Division. It was now the Premier League.

BskyB beat off ITV for the live television rights with the BBC securing highlights with Match of the Day. Clubs were happy as they would rake in £1.5m a year. A "whole new ball game" was promised by BskyB with Simple Minds "Alive and kicking" sound tracking the promo that was busy hyping it up. The idea of two live matches a week sounded great, but hardly anyone had the satellite dish needed. This meant our new sponsors, Tulip, were not pleased with the amount of coverage they would get. Some details were given to fans at the popular Palace Open Day, most non-armchair supporters resented the changes to kick off times for TV.

England were hopeless at the Euros, going out after a dire 2-1 defeat to Sweden with Tomas Brolin scoring the winner. Palace would have a comedy season with him at centre stage a few years later.

There was speculation that Arsenal, and wealthy newly promoted Blackburn, wanted Geoff Thomas, so Palace promptly put a £4m price tag on him. One transfer sadly concluded, Andy Gray converting his loan to Spurs to a permanent switch. Meanwhile Andy Thorn thankfully signed a new deal but the quality forward we craved remained elusive. This was despite reported interest in Brian Deane again, Kevin Gallagher at Coventry, and Duncan Ferguson at Dundee United. Instead, the only incomer was Darren Patterson a £200,000 defender from Wigan whilst a move for full back Terry Phelan fizzled out. It was a wonder Gary Bennett wasn't mentioned again. Despite these reports clubcall indicated Palace are more likely to rely on young players coming through.

Our five a side team had started playing in numerous events including a trip to Huddersfield. We got there the night before to prepare for a tournament featuring Leeds United's impressive youth team. Our preparation wasn't as professional as it could have been. Many beers in the Zetland were followed by a lock-in which ended with a game of running in a circle with a broom attached to your head. The first injury of the weekend occurred when Clubby slipped, cut his head and ended up in A&E. I was more worried about who would play at the back than his welfare. Later that summer we played at Carshalton. I drove having picked up the man mountain Andy "Wags" Wagon who was a useful striker. We had to stop three times so he could chuck up after the previous night's refreshment. Somehow, we made the final. Steve Coppell never had to cope with these issues. Well, hopefully not.

I was worried about how many games I would get to for the coming season. There were to be redundancies at work, and I was the first to be called in to see the new TACA chairman. I looked at Andy and said, "oh well, I'm off then." Instead, I was told there was an opening in the accounts department and was I interested. Yes, I said. I was on the path to becoming a qualified accountant, and my plans to get to all Palace matches were not changed after all.

Palace's pre-season started with the usual one-sided victories in Sweden, plus a win in pouring rain at Brighton (always a joy) and another at Orient.

Blackburn Rovers had come up thanks to considerable funding from Jack Walker who said he would pay "whatever it took" to get Blackburn to the top and had signed Alan Shearer and a host of other players to set them on their way. It would be a tough opener in warm sunshine. In a tight first half a near post header from Bright gave us the lead but Ripley equalised following poor marking just before half time. Southgate put us ahead again with his first league goal but then Shearer showed why he was worth the £3.6m price tag and fired in two crackers in front of the Holmesdale. The game looked lost until little Simon Osborn popped up with a header to get us a point. An excellent game. Thomas was expected to join Rovers after the game and clearly found the situation strange "I don't feel like a Palace player, I don't feel like a Blackburn player." He remained with us, for now at least.

We drew at Oldham in the week, although the TV screen broke down so I could only enjoy the first ten minutes of "Who framed Roger Rabbit" on the coach. I did meet Rob, Adrian and Dave in the ground and saw a dire first half with little attacking threat which wasn't surprising with Bright missing and Salako picking up an injury. McGoldrick slotted home an equaliser to make the prompt journey home more enjoyable, particularly as it seemed Thomas's move to Blackburn had collapsed.

Steve Coppell was not an early fan of the Premier League "They have useless administration, are a complete waste of time, and only care about money. They have all these fabulous plans but don't care about some of the teams, the big clubs are just saying sod you."

My £5.15 capital card got me to a feisty draw at Spurs. The niggly atmosphere was not helped by referee Philip Don. He harshly penalised Martyn for apparently taking more than four steps, then booked Thorn when he encroached as Samways faked to take the free kick. When Samways did the same thing again, instead of booking our latest encroachers he booked Samways. Later he sent off both Ruddock and Thorn following a hard but fair challenge, as they got up they caught each other with no apparent malice but Don saw fit to show them both red cards. A late Sedgley goal meant the game finished 2-2. Gray was only on the bench which seemed strange, but he got some stick from the Palace crowd anyway. Ruddock would have a poor spell with us a few years later, but his teammate David Tuttle would prove more popular at Selhurst during the nineties.

A dull evening game followed against Sheffield Wednesday, a 1-1 draw with Young scoring as he had at Spurs, but a rare Martyn error gifting an equaliser. Sitting again in row 35 of the Arthur Wait my Dad and I started to worry about how this season would pan out. Those fears were not eased on the Saturday as we lost 2-1 to Norwich, a match we needed to win to avoid dropping to the lower end of the table. It felt like a crisis. Chris Coleman was still a makeshift forward when we surely needed a new signing. We got one when Chris Armstrong joined for £1.5m from Millwall. He needed to be an instant success not least as crowds were getting worse, down to just 12,000. "We've lost our spirit" warned Thomas.

Dave, Adrian, Rob, and I got the 12.30pm coach to Old Trafford hoping for a point, and we nearly got it. After 89 minutes Hughes latched on to McClair's pass to win it for them, earlier an Eric Young challenge had broken Dion Dublin's leg. It was a long trip home, but we did have the benefit of a pub stop at least. Armstrong had a decent debut, but we still hadn't won this season. That continued at Villa with a 3-0 defeat. We started very brightly and did dominate patches of the game which led Ron Atkinson to concede that their keeper, Nigel Spink, was man of the match. Stuart Massey came on as sub, the following year we were playing five a side against him.

Our prospects took another grim turn when Mark Bright joined Sheffield Wednesday for £350,000 plus nippy forward Paul Williams. He and Armstrong needed to work out and the pair would give us some pace up top now. Leicester moaned that the deal, valued at £850,000, had been manipulated so they didn't get their full cut as part of the original deal when Bright joined us. Many suspected it was another of Noades's cunning plans to save us some cash.

Our lowest Saturday home crowd since 1989 of 11,224 welcomed Oldham and it felt like a must win match. We drew. Having gone behind the atmosphere was grim at half time, but new boy Armstrong scored twice in a minute to put us ahead. At last a win I thought. Wrong. A late Kevin Sharp goal made it 2-2. It felt like a kick in the teeth and left only Forest below us. Big problems now.

Armstrong scored twice again the following week and had a storming game to, glory be, get us three points at Everton. Having celebrated that for a bit too long Dave and I missed the 5.15 train home so enjoyed a beer and a pizza, before getting the later one, only to be sat opposite a guy with his Walkman on so loud I could hear him playing the Shaman's "Ebenezer Goode" on loop.

The joy at that win, and the hope it would lead to better times were dashed at home to Southampton. We dominated the match throughout and the Saints goal led a charmed life including Salako's penalty hitting the post, typically Dowie put them ahead with their only chance of the first half. Young equalised, but Dowie then got a gutting winner in the 88th minute. A sickening defeat as a win would have lifted us towards mid table. We were back to being just one off the bottom. Salako summed up how everyone felt "I want to go home and cry after that." Paper reports said Inspector Morse would have nicked Southampton for daylight robbery.

Andy and I booked a guest house for a trip to Coventry, we knew how to glam it up particularly as it rained torrentially all day. Palace played well and drew 2-2 on a sodden pitch. The following day we saw Andy's Hammers draw 0-0 at Wolves, with Julian Dicks being sent off following a fracas that saw the sizeable figure of Billy Bonds racing up the touchline looking like he was desperate to get involved in a scrap as well.

Our trip to Lincoln in the league (Coca-Cola) cup saw us complete a 4-2 aggregate win. The following day I received a lengthy letter from the Department of National Heritage after I had written to them with concerns over supporters being priced out of football if grounds went all seater. It wasn't particularly understanding of these concerns.

We had another home game riddled with frustration. Yet again we had the better of it against Manchester City, but the game ended goalless. Early on Williams got the better of Curle and set Armstrong up who sliced a shot halfway up the Holmesdale. The defeat left us still one place off the bottom. It was clear we were in a relegation battle and the glories of our third-place finish just two seasons ago seemed a distant memory.

A lively match followed at Ipswich where in constant rain we watched from an excellent vantage point high on the halfway line. It was 2-2 as the game moved deep into injury time when we got a dodgy penalty for handball. The tension was immense in the Palace end. What a chance to pull clear of the bottom three. Too many draws! Southgate stepped up and slammed the penalty against the post. Gutted. We headed back to London to meet Andy where many beers were sank in the smoky Globe and Allsop Arms.

We got to the fourth round of the League cup with a win at Southampton, some revenge for the league defeat when we seemed to play with so much tension.

BskyB had introduced a few gimmicks for their Monday night football coverage. One of these involved two massive inflatable wrestlers grappling in the centre circle at half time. Very bizarre. Other aspects of it were very good: vastly improved sound around the ground, dancers and fireworks livening up a chilly evening. We were playing Arsenal and, despite McGoldrick equalising Merson's opener, we lost by conceding a winner on 73 minutes, inevitably scored by Wright. We missed his quality so much.

Life got no better at Chelsea, a 3-1 defeat watched in despair with Robbie and Andy "Essex" Curtis. The early own goal from Richard Shaw set the scene for another forgettable afternoon.

We remembered even less when the Baker Street pubs came into play once more. Assistant manager Alan Smith was worried our players were too nice and was keen for the likes of Osborne, Williams, Salako and Southgate to become tougher. It was now our worst start for 19 years. The following weekend Andy and I went to see bitter rivals Brighton have a lucky win over Hayes in the FA Cup and then went to a "lively" fixture - Millwall v West Ham, not one for the faint-hearted. Andy was unimpressed with a 2-1 defeat. I thought it best not to point out that former Palace man Phil Barber got Millwall's first.

We faced a bottom of the table clash against Forest the following week. Having led through Armstrong we conceded a late equaliser to make it ten home league games without a win. After the game Palace were apparently opening the doors to Yugoslav international midfielder Stanojkovic, with a potential £150,000 deal weirdly instigated by DJ Dave "Kid" Jensen. The deal collapsed. Far more disappointing was the news that John Salako would miss the rest of the season thanks to his injured left knee. With Bright sold and Williams not scoring we looked thin on options up front.

The optimism for the Liverpool trip wasn't too high, as Dave, Robbie and I headed to Anfield on the £17.50 inter-city. We were slaughtered. Being three down in seventeen minutes brought back memories of the 9-0 but this time they settled for five, as pressure began to build on Coppell. The train trip was broken at Crewe where we found an excellent hotel for a couple of beers, and a few cans for the rest of the journey that started a feud when people were in our prebooked seats, Dave asked them to move and was then labelled "uppity and smug" by a woman with a Liverpool top on. We did get to enjoy the £2.80 new pizza pasta all-you-can-eat buffet in Victoria, I felt a little sick on the way home having gained full value out of it.

During the week, disillusioned at not being able to make the breakthrough into the team, Stan Collymore left to join

Southend for £200,000. With resources so limited up front it seemed strange to let him leave, but there hadn't been much clamour from the supporters either for him to have further chances after his fleeting substitute appearances. Meanwhile Ron Noades upped the pressure on Coppell blasting the team as "unprofessional, slipshod and complacent." The mood was not good.

We went back to Anfield in the fourth round of the League cup just three days later. The coach happily letting Dave, Rob, Dave and Adrian and I frequent the Greyhound in Stafford on the way up where we were greeted with great northern hospitality by the barman "Waste of time you boys even coming up, we'll score more than five this time." It looked like a second half diving header from Coleman would give us a shock win, but Jones fell over in the box and Liverpool got a very soft penalty to get a replay at Selhurst. It was a great effort, and the team showed way more spirit than recent weeks particularly with youngsters Ndah and Bowry getting a start. Liverpool boss Souness wasn't too chuffed and clearly thought Palace had been over physical. Alan Smith disputed that "Ronnie Moran shook my hand and said we had done really well, as did the Liverpool directors."

We had to beat Sheffield United on Saturday 5 December or we would be about six points adrift from the safety of 19th. After four minutes former target Deane thought he had the ball over the line, but the referee waved play on. TV replays proved it clearly went in. Some luck at last I thought! We took full advantage with Armstrong and Southgate scoring to give us the win. Still one-off bottom, but not marooned. It was also good news that Geoff Thomas was set to return from injury. The upturn continued at QPR, who dominated the first half, but three second half goals gave us a second consecutive win. I celebrated only modestly in the pub afterwards following the TACA office Christmas do where I had drunk way too much champagne the previous night. First world problems.

Nobody expected us to get past Liverpool in the cup replay but an early goal from young Grant Watts gave us hope, but Marsh put a penalty away and we headed into extra-time. The thought of another trip to Liverpool beckoned for a second replay but Thorn headed us ahead. We held on against the likes of Rush, Barnes, McManaman and Rosenthal and would play Chelsea at Selhurst in the Quarter-Final. We all felt it justice for the "Anfield" penalty Liverpool got in the first game.

We faced another top team the following Sunday in champions Leeds, Thorn getting the winner again with a 29th minute header. Then on a chilly Boxing Day we beat fellow strugglers Wimbledon with first half goals. We were now out of the dreaded bottom three at long last and were even top of the current form table.

The trip to Middlesbrough was bitterly cold. We caught the 9.30 inter-city and arrived at 1pm in a howling gale. A free bus took us close to the ground, but I didn't fancy waiting nearly two hours in sub-zero temperatures so managed to sneakily escape the strict police escort and found a local pub. I chatted to a few locals for a bit then left at 2.45 and met the others who were turning blue. I explained where the pub was, and immediately the steward said, "You were lucky mate, that's a rough place." Palace struggled on the pitch and it seemed only a matter of time until they scored. Martyn made a series of spectacular saves, each one better than the last. Midway through the second half Osborne put us ahead with a shot from the edge of the box and although it didn't seem possible the pressure built even further on our goal but thanks to Martyn, Thorn and Young we got three points to take us up to 15th.

On New Year's Eve 1992 Andy and I were optimistic. He that West Ham would come back up, and I that Palace had overcome an awful start to the season despite losing Bright. With Armstrong finding form, and us rising up the table, I hoped we could get to close to our midtable final position of last season. With no Salako thanks to the injury, and Williams not finding the net, there was not a lot of depth behind an inexperienced striker. I kept hoping we would sign another forward but with crowds falling that seemed unlikely. We both looked forward to Palace v West Ham clashes in the Premier League next season.

Having already endured a coach trip to Hartlepool last season I didn't fancy a repeat for the FA Cup tie particularly as British Rail couldn't offer discounted rates over the holiday period and a return was £68. As well as that the forecast was for icy weather so the game may well be off. Instead, I joined Andy for his drive to WBA to see West Ham cruise to a 2-0 win in dense fog. I had my ear pinned to my Walkman, an upscale one that included a radio! Andy spent much of the afternoon asking, "have Hartlepool scored yet?" Confidently I kept saying "of course not". But on 83 minutes they got a soft penalty given by Dermot Gallagher (who rarely did us any favours) after a succession of corners. Andy turned towards me again "Have Hartlepool scored yet?" "Um, yes I said." He giggled. I frowned. Coppell did not approve, "There'd be six penalties a game if they are to be given for that." At least Andy was driving so I could down a few pints as we stopped at the splendid Beefeater just off the M40. Andy enjoyed the extensive Match of the Day highlights from the Victoria ground more than I did, or presumably Richard Shaw who committed the "foul" to give them the penalty.

We needed a lift after that in the League cup quarter final against Chelsea. The weather was incredibly wet, it chucked it down all day and it seemed likely the match would be postponed, but half an hour before the start it got the go ahead. We couldn't use Armstrong as he was cup-tied so young Grant Watts got another start against a very experienced Chelsea team. The sodden conditions helped us out, a dreadful back pass from Sinclair stopped in one of many puddles and Coleman slid in on the edge of the box to guide the ball past Hitchcock. Everyone celebrated wildly but the ball only just crawled through the standing water and over the line. The mightily impressive Townsend equalised, but a flick on from Young was kept in play by Thorn and young "Ooh Aah" George Ndah scrambled it over the line, and we took a lead into half time. It was a classic first half, in ridiculous conditions but it made for compulsive viewing. Just after half time Watts seemed to slip but managed to direct a cross past Hitchcock and we now led 3-1. Chelsea faded after a fine double save by Martyn and we clung on, drenched, on a classic night at Selhurst. "Some people said we lacked character after Hartlepool, they got it wrong. We have bags of spirit here." said Coppell. We would face Arsenal in a two-legged semi-final. A tough run if we are to get to the final then, Liverpool followed by Chelsea followed by Arsenal!

The mood now was far more positive, with McGoldrick playing so well at sweeper he got the Evening Standard player of the month. We were rising up the league and had a cup semi-final to look forward to.

That came to a juddering halt at home to Everton who won with two second half goals leaving Coppell to admit "We were rubbish." We were still five points clear of the relegation zone at least, and had five young players in the line-up, Bowry, Newman, Watts, Ndah and Rodger. Nobody could be sure if they would be consistently Premier League quality players, and I sat freezing at East Croydon station thinking how we missed Wright, Bright, Gray and the injured Salako. We were no better at Southampton, losing a poor game 1-0. We moved McGoldrick up front towards the end, but our high balls were just headed out by the impressive Monkou. Robbie, Paul, and I sensed the relegation worries pre-Christmas were returning. I was keen for McGoldrick to stay up front. Young and Thorn shouldn't need a sweeper except in exceptional situations and we were lacking a goal threat, even more so with Williams still out so not giving us any value following the departure of Bright.

On the Wednesday, the team went to Norwich, but I followed it first on Ceefax then on Capital Gold with commentary saying how well Norwich had played, but it was 2-2 at the break. They added a third quickly and as I moved back to Ceefax, I stared at the screen hoping for the screen to flash round to 3-3. It went to 4-2 instead then the dreaded "result" appeared. On the Saturday we produced a disastrous first half and were three down by half time against Spurs with even Andy Gray scoring to make it seem that little bit worse. We looked like clueless kids. Coppell realised it had been terrible "I apologise to our fans; the buck stops with me." We were now back in the relegation zone. A Ruddock own goal was no consolation.

Next was an evening trip to big spending fifth placed Blackburn. It wasn't promising! I decided to play five a side and expected news of a depressing defeat. We sat in Crawley's White Knight when I went out to my car to check the score. The Capital Gold commentary seemed to be in the Palace end, and you could hear general chit chat as well "Oy Mick, just gonna get a pie." Eventually I heard "score remains 1-1 ten minutes into the second half". Ooh that's good I thought. I went back to the pub and hoped for the best. Then our five-a-side new signing Ian Fletcher's wife Cheryl came over and said, "Its 2-1." We groaned. "To Palace!" We grinned, looked shocked, and checked our watches. We held on. Both our goals from Armstrong and Rodger were classics and put us five points clear of the relegation zone. An unexpected three points that were desperately needed.

It certainly gave us a lift for the first leg of the Coca-Cola (League) Cup Semi-Final against Arsenal at Selhurst. My Dad and I planned to get the 1.30 train but after standing on the Three Bridges platform for ages it was announced that trains were suddenly cancelled for engineering works. We got refunds and Dad dashed back and got the car. We drove up with an Arsenal fan who was also marooned. Parking was a pain, so Dad kindly dropped me and Mr Arsenal off and he missed the first few minutes. He arrived to see Wright put

Arsenal in front from the spot after ten minutes and when Smith made it 2-0, we knew the tie was surely over after only twenty minutes. Lee Sinnott had a poor game and was told this very clearly by the Arthur Wait stand. We ended up losing 3-1 with Coppell admitting his man to man marking tactic on Wright hadn't worked.

We got a win on the Wednesday with Bowry scoring the only goal after nine minutes against Villa. We scored, sat back, and defended well. I thought I would be due at work before the referee ended the never-ending injury time as devilish corners threatened our goal. The energetic Bowry had been nicknamed "Somalia" due to his very small frame and Coppell admitted after the game "the kid looked so ill, I thought he'd need an oxygen tank."

I travelled to Sheffield Wednesday with Dave and his mate Ian, a Wednesday fan. We sat opposite a woman who seemed to take an instant dislike to us as she headed home. She tutted when a newspaper went just into her quarter of the table, tutted when Ian started eating, tutted when I asked if I could squeeze by to go to the toilet, tutted when Dave opened a cider. We decided to wind her up a bit and began comments such as "trouble down pit" "Ee up chuck, where's me barm cake" or "Wont owt from buffet". She tutted. We got our comeuppance at the game, being awful in the first half and lucky to be just one down. The start of the second half was a vast improvement culminating in Armstrong beating the offside trap to level. Sadly, the former Brighton midfield Danny Wilson sickeningly got their winner after Martyn made a cock up of a back pass and we headed to the longest bar in England, the Stonehouse, for a few drinks for us, and Ken the pen.

There are certain games you dread when the fixtures come out on a sunny day in the summer. Coventry at home is one. It is generally full of frustration, cold weather and a low crowd. We drew 0-0 and it was just that. We got another draw, this time at improving Forest with Southgate's deflected shot being equalised by Roy Keane. I had been driven up in Paul's car with and Dave. We had drinks before, then after in the Aviary pub which made the non-stop journey back "challenging."

ITV had clearly decided we had no chance in the second leg of the semi-final. They had the rights to show it live but abandoned that for Coronation Street and we just had a half hour highlights show. They were right as Arsenal won 2-0.

Most Palace v Chelsea games had been gripping affairs but the latest didn't carry on the trend, presumably much to Sky's chagrin. We seemed to be in a let's-get-set- plays-and-not-bother-with-any-ideas mood. Chelsea should have won the 1-1 draw, they had gone ahead after Stuart's shot bobbled past Martyn only for Armstrong's excellent header to equalise. That goal increased his profile and Benfica were said to be interested. One who wasn't leaving was Coppell who made his position very clear "I am not leaving, come what may – stories that suggest I am are just bull. I am committed to this club for 18 months and have no intention of quitting." Despite the struggles of the season that was reassuring to most particularly as Noades said he had no interest in looking for a new manager, and instead changed topics to make it clear he was disappointed Bright didn't stay longer to help young Armstrong.

The trip to Sheffield United was a big game as they were fellow strugglers and Coppell rightly predicted a scrap, particularly as the club were indicating they would "sell big" if we went down. I caught the 11.30 on my own but met Gary on the way up then the usual crew in the ground. It was looking bleak when Armstrong was sent off, but a brave Coleman header put us ahead in a feisty first half. The second was backs-to-the-wall stuff with Young and Thorn at their best and if they got past them Martyn showed his class yet again. It was a vital win and the cans of lager tasted so much better than they did on the way home from Sheffield a few weeks ago. When we picked the Sunday papers up at Victoria, we found we had signed striker Louie Donowa and keeper Martin Thomas on loan until the end of the season. Meanwhile Collymore, who had looked fantastic at Southend, was being linked with a £2m move to Forest. He and Armstrong could have formed a very handy partnership, and if we had kept Bright too that would be a cracking forward line. Oh well.

Liverpool arrived on the following Tuesday and played some excellent football and when Rush put them ahead it looked bleak for us, but a late Armstrong goal got us a precious equaliser. That left manager Souness moaning for Scotland and the crowd loved it when referee Dilkes went over and gave him a good telling off and then sent him off. He may have had a point though when Rush had a goal disallowed for a very dodgy offside decision. Oh well, they have had a few decisions at Anfield I reckoned!

There was a testimonial for Malcolm Allision on an international Saturday. A lively afternoon with a Palace v Legends seven a side and an 80-minute first team match against Spurs which ended 3-3. Sadly only 1,600 showed up.

A poor game followed at home to QPR. Bradley Allen put Rangers ahead and we needed an own goal to get a point. That day the Grand National was cancelled, many punters wished this had been too.

Good Friday was shocking. We sat in the Arthur Wait for the "away" game against Wimbledon and Sky covered our 4-0 thrashing in torrential rain. It was desperate and having got so close to pulling away from the relegation scrap we were now just one place above the bottom three. We needed a few beers in Baker Street to get over this fiasco. The Easter Monday game against near bottom Middlesbrough was now critical, and this time we turned up. A massive band gave it sense of occasion, the sun shone, and after showing promise in the first half we slammed in four second half goals to win 4-1. We were lucky with the first, a deflected Rodger free kick but then we were clinical enough to take advantage of some poor defending, which was very welcome. That put us five points clear and I celebrated that with a few beers in Crowborough with Andy who was less chuffed as West Ham had lost at Luton.

We were shocked it would cost £26 to get to Leeds but still seven of us made our way hoping for a point against a team who had only lost once at home all season. It was a tight game but thanks to the ever-reliable Thorn and Young partnership we ground out a draw which I was delighted with. A golden point I thought, and still five points clear with another game gone. We had a few giggles on the way home, not least with some naughty girls who got on our train with no tickets. We wound them up relentlessly with "here comes the ticket inspector" and watched the panic set in as we smugly waved our tickets around.

A massive crowd of 30,115 turned up and saw Manchester United get even closer to their first championship since the sixties with second half Hughes and Ince goals. We competed well though with Young outstanding, and the crowd enjoyed Coleman's "vigorous" challenge on Schmeichel. United fans were even happier when closest rivals, Villa, lost.

I knew the United game was a distraction. The big one was against fellow strugglers Ipswich. Win this and we would be all but safe. It was a warm and sunny day and a good crowd of nearly 19,000 were in good spirits. So many home games this season had been poor, not just the results but the performances. However now, when it really mattered, we produced a cracking start full of energy and determination. After a spell of pressure Coleman won the ball off Milton and forced a corner and Young prodded the ball over the line. With our confidence up Armstrong broke away and slammed a shot against the post, then two minutes later a surge forward by Southgate ended with the ball arriving at McGoldrick's feet who crossed for Armstrong to bundle it in. Ipswich pulled one back when Gregory scored from old man Wark's cross, and we knew the second half would be tense. The stress was eased when Williams excellent pass was clinically put away by McGoldrick in front of the Whitehorse. The whistle went and under blue skies the players did a lap of honour. The only way we could go down was to get less than two points at Manchester City and Arsenal, whilst Oldham also had to win all three of their matches including away at championship chasing Villa then home to Liverpool and Southampton. The chances of that happening were so remote, but it was a nagging worry. I had plenty of beers to celebrate us being eight points clear of the only team that could catch us with a week to go and woke groggily to REM's "Losing my religion" the following day feeling relived that we had surely survived and could look to strengthen for next season.

The following day my Mum, Dad and I went out for the day. I looked forward to getting home to find Oldham hadn't won at second placed, and championship chasing, Villa so our safety would be secured. I walked through the door and put Ceefax on to see "Aston Villa 0 Oldham 1. Full time." My heart skipped a beat. Oh no. The tension had returned.

If we won at City that would make us safe. I was tempted to go but it was Andy's birthday, so we did a pub crawl around Crawley ending up in The Plough in Three Bridges where there was a small TV with Ceefax showing the football scores. It said 0-0. "That's OK?" asked Andy. "Not really, a point makes little difference." Not least as Oldham were beating Liverpool 3-2. We needed either a Liverpool goal, or a Palace goal and we would be safe. I stared at the screen for the last ten minutes, but the dreaded "Full time" appeared by both. This meant we needed a draw at Arsenal to stay up, if we lost, we would have to rely on Oldham not beating Southampton at home. What a contrast to the relief we all felt just four days earlier during the Selhurst lap of honour.

Our record at Arsenal was shocking. They were a top team, and we would have to play a perfect game to get a result, and hope they had an off day, or took it easy before their cup final next week. All the usuals showed up including Andy whose West Ham were already promoted, hopefully to meet us next season. Straight from the kick-off it was clear Arsenal were not saving themselves at all, and our old boy Wright put them ahead after 9 minutes. Realistically we were now left hoping that somehow Southampton could get a result at Oldham but half an hour in and Oldham scored. Everyone just looked at the floor. Then "Boys, 1-1 Le Tissier has scored for Saints." We were back in the it, until Oldham scored again on the stroke of half time. We started the second half well, Young and Southgate going close as we prayed for an equaliser particularly as we heard Oldham now led 4-1. Arsenal scored again through Dickov and some started to get tearful in the away end. There was news though that Southampton had scored twice and with five minutes to go it was 4-3. Hope. We prayed for a miraculous equaliser for Southampton, 1976 would be forgotten I thought. Arsenal added a third. The news came through that Oldham had won. The ref blew up at Highbury and that was it. We were relegated. It seemed so final. So brutal.

It was a shattering and numbing experience. Coppell ran down the tunnel and told reporters that the players were inconsolable "Nobody can say a word". Wright was not popular now with the Palace crowd with one particularly nasty chant aimed at him, but he did say "They say you can't score a bad goal, but I managed to do it today. To say I'm disappointed is an understatement but I had to do my job." Coppell was unsure what the future held and was worried his players would be open to the vultures. There were quite a few who would be attractive in the market – Martyn, Young, Thorn, Thomas, Armstrong, Shaw, Salako, McGoldrick, Coleman, Southgate for sure which made me think we should have had enough not to get relegated despite Salako's injury. It becomes very difficult when you sell your best players and we had lost three legends in Bright, Wright and Gray and hadn't adequately replaced them. Only Armstrong of the signings since and the youngsters coming through had been a great success. I had realised that a club of our size will always struggle to replace our top players with those of a similar ability.

We made our quiet way out of the grandiose setting of Highbury with people consoling each other whether they were friends or not, wondering where our next game would be. "Stockport or Port Vale?" suggested Andy. We all headed for Victoria and had a few beers in the Duke of York. We felt gloomy and despite a little black humour it was a very quiet hour reflecting on where we go from here. Nobody could be sure.

After years of chasing and gaining promotion, staying up in the first year, getting to a cup final, finishing as the third best team in the country and winning the ZDS a fabulous era had ended. We were back to where we started in August 1981.

The others left. Andy and I finished our pints, with me still nearly speechless. He looked at me and said, "Come on, let's go for a curry and a couple of large cobras."

I smiled for the first time since kick-off.

"Good plan mate."

Epilogue

With 49 points we were very unlucky to go down in 1993, as we proved the following season by coming straight back up as champions with Alan Smith replacing Coppell. We lost Thomas and McGoldrick but kept enough quality to easily get promoted particularly once the experience of Paul Stewart arrived on loan to give us a boost from Christmas. However, we came straight back down again.

Having lost to a last-minute goal from Claridge in the 1996 play-off final, we got back up again in 1997 with Hopkin getting a memorable winner in the following years Wembley stress-a-thon. Incredibly we then added a true star of European football, Attilio Lombardo, but an ill-fated season followed so again we were relegated after a single season. Staying up just seemed impossible.

Mark Goldberg had purchased the club from Noades, and promptly installed Terry Venables for a brief second spell in 1997. Eventually the club passed to Simon Jordan in 2000.

We beat Andy's West Ham in a play-off final in 2004 and got close to staying up the following season. Playing Southampton in the last home game we needed to win and were a goal ahead. Southampton got a very late free kick. "I can't see Southampton scoring." I said. Southampton scored. I got severely and deservedly glared at. We went down the next week at gloating Charlton.

The latest financial crisis in 2010 was eased with a takeover led by Steve Parish with the club on the verge of liquidating.

A typically tense play off saw us promoted again in 2013, and three years later we got to another cup final and led again against Manchester United. I can't think of another club who has led twice in two cup finals and has not won it. I pray we go one better someday.

As I write this in 2021, we are now in our eighth successive season in the Premier League with Wilf Zaha the best I have seen in a Palace shirt. I have learned from supporting us for so long that we must appreciate the good times. It can take a very long time for a club of our standing to reach where we are now, and it is equally tough to maintain it with our resources. The efforts of all who do should be very much appreciated.

I stopped going to as many away games as the nineties went on. Instead, I went on various England cricket tours. They were all fantastic, very different to travelling around in the cold watching Palace for sure. I am though still a season ticket holder and go to a few away games each season and will do for decades to come all being well.

With Palace who knows what's ahead!

Statistics August 1981 to May 1993

Appearances

Cannon	319
Barber	287
Bright	286
Wright	277
Thomas	249
Wood	221
Gray	191
Martyn	190
McGoldrick	188
Salako	177
Nebbeling	173
Pardew	166
Thorn	156
Shaw	152
Murphy	144
Hilaire	140
Hughton	137
Young	137
Humphrey	136
Irvine	127
Stebbing	118
Finnigan	118
Gilbert	115
Pemberton	105
Locke	101
Giles	100
Taylor	99
Burke	97
Hopkins	93
Mabbutt	88
O'Reilly	85
Southgate	81
Hinchelwood	75
Sparrow	73
Barron	71
Ketteridge	71
Suckling	71
Coleman	70
Sinnott	67
Redfearn	65
Osborne	65
Langley	62
Aylott	61
Lovell	59
Droy	58
Rodger	58
Brush	56
Nicholas	55
O'Doherty	51
Smillie	50
Brooks	47
Pennyfather	41
Armstrong	36
Cummins	34
Madden	33

Appearances (continued)

Fry	31	Galliers	13
Lacy	30	Wilkins	13
Higginbottom	30	Williams	13
McCulloch	29	Brown	11
Dyer	27	Hodges	11
Price	26	Dennis	10
Hedman	26	Bodin	10
Mortimer	26	Hughes, B	9
Edwards	25	Watts	8
Lindsay	25	Strong	7
Parkin	25	Galloway	6
Gabbiadini	25	Moralee	6
Mahoney	24	Dare	5
Collymore	24	Howe	5
Evans	23	Bailey	5
Bason	22	Powell	5
Boulter	22	Leahy	4
Jones	22	Howard	4
Thompson	22	Hardwick	3
Williams	21	Hone	3
Wicks	19	Fashanu	2
Ndah	18	Harris	2
Walsh	17	Newman	2
Whyte	17	Baxter	1
Gordon	17	Martin	1
Whyte	16	Barnes	1
Bowry	16	Sullivan	1
Otulakowski	14	Massey	1
		Hughes, K	1

Goal scorers

Wright	117
Bright	113
Gray	51
Barber	41
Thomas	35
Mabbutt	24
Salako	19
Hilaire	17
Cannon	16
McGoldrick	16
Armstrong	15
Taylor	15
Aylott	14
Irvine	14
Pardew	12
Young	12
Coleman	11
Hinchelwood	11
Murphy	11
Finnigan	10
Redfearn	10
Cummins	8
Nebbeling	8
Nicholas	8
Droy	7
Edwards	7

Evans	7
Gabbiadini	7
Langley	7
Giles	6
Ketteridge	6
Madden	6
Thorn	6
Brooks	5
Dyer	5
Mahoney	5
Osborne	5
Southgate	5
Hopkins	4
McCulloch	4
O'Reilly	4
Smillie	4
Thompson	4
Brush	3
Jones	3
Lovell	3
Stebbing	3
Wilkins	3
Brown	2
Collymore	2
Gilbert	2
Higginbottom	2
Mortimer	2

Goal scorers (continued)

Pemberton	2
Rodger	2
Sparrow	2
Walsh	2
Watts	2
Whyte	2
Bailey	1
Bowry	1
Galloway	1
Hodges	1
Hughton	1
Humphrey	1
Locke	1
Ndah	1
O'Doherty	1
Otulakowski	1
Pennyfather	1
Price	1
Shaw	1
Wicks	1

Playing Record and Attendances

Season	Played	Won	Drew	Lost	Goals For	Goals Against	League Position
Division Two:							
1981/82	51	18	10	23	43	52	15th
1982/83	51	17	14	20	54	58	15th
1983/84	47	14	13	20	47	57	18th
1984/85	48	13	15	20	50	70	15th
1985/86	49	20	10	19	65	63	5th
1986/87	49	21	7	21	55	64	6th
1987/88	49	24	9	16	93	63	6th
1988/89	59	31	12	16	95	68	3rd
Division One:							
1989/90	54	22	11	21	68	88	15th
1990/91	52	28	13	11	77	53	3rd
1991/92	54	19	19	16	75	77	10th
1992/93	51	15	18	18	61	72	20th

Cup Record (Round reached)

Season	F.A.	League*	FM**
1981/82	Quarter-Final	4th	n/a
1982/83	5th	3rd	n/a
1983/84	4th	1st	n/a
1984/85	3rd	2nd	n/a
1985/86	3rd	2nd	1st
1986/87	4th	3rd	1st
1987/88	3rd	3rd	1st
1988/89	3rd	3rd	Semi-Final
1989/90	Final	3rd	Semi-Final
1990/91	3rd	4th	Winners
1991/92	3rd	Quarter-Final	Quarter-Final
1992/93	3rd	Semi-Final	n/a

* Sponsored by the Milk Marketing Board, Littlewoods, Rumbelows and Coca Cola.
** Sponsored by Simod and Zenith Data Systems.

Average Home League Attendances

Season	Attendance	Season	Attendance
1981/82	10,030	1987/88	9,746
1982/83	9,887	1988/89	10,655
1983/84	8,199	1989/90	17,105
1984/85	6,440	1990/91	19,660
1985/86	6,788	1991/92	17,619
1986/87	7,583	1992/93	15,748

Printed in Great Britain
by Amazon